Gary Soto

WHO WROTE THAT?

LOUISA MAY ALCOTT
JANE AUSTEN
AVI
JUDY BLUME
BETSY BYARS
BEVERLY CLEARY
ROBERT CORMIER
BRUCE COVILLE
ROALD DAHL
CHARLES DICKENS
THEODOR GEISEL
WILL HOBBS
ANTHONY HOROWITZ
GAIL CARSON LEVINE
C.S. LEWIS
ANN M. MARTIN
L.M. MONTGOMERY
PAT MORA
WALTER DEAN MYERS
SCOTT O'DELL
BARBARA PARK
GARY PAULSEN
TAMORA PIERCE
EDGAR ALLAN POE
BEATRIX POTTER
PHILIP PULLMAN
MYTHMAKER: THE STORY OF J.K. ROWLING
MAURICE SENDAK
SHEL SILVERSTEIN
GARY SOTO
R.L. STINE
EDWARD L. STRATEMEYER
E.B. WHITE
LAURA INGALLS WILDER
LAURENCE YEP
JANE YOLEN

WHO WROTE THAT?

Gary Soto

Dennis Abrams

Foreword by
Kyle Zimmer

CHELSEA HOUSE PUBLISHERS
An imprint of Infobase Publishing

Gary Soto

Chelsea House
An imprint of Infobase Publishing
132 West 31st Street
New York NY 10001

Library of Congress Cataloging-in-Publication Data
Abrams, Dennis.
Gary Soto / Dennis Abrams.
p. cm. — (Who wrote that?)
Includes bibliographical references and index.
ISBN 978-0-7910-9529-4 (hardcover)
1. Soto, Gary. 2. Authors, American—20th century—Biography. 3. Authors, American—21st century—Biography. 4. Mexican American authors—Biography. I. Title. II. Series.
PS3569.O72Z53 2008
811'.54—dc22
[B] 2007045509

Chelsea House books are available at special discounts when purchased in bulk quantities for business, associations, institutions, or sales promotions. Please call our Special Sales Department in New York at (212) 967-8800 or (800) 322-8755.

You can find Chelsea House on the World Wide Web at http://www.chelseahouse.com

Text design by Keith Trego and Erika Arroyo
Cover design by Keith Trego and Jooyoung An

Printed in the United States of America

Bang EJB 10 9 8 7 6 5 4 3 2 1

This book is printed on acid-free paper.

Table of Contents

FOREWORD BY
KYLE ZIMMER
PRESIDENT, FIRST BOOK

HUMANITY IS POWERED by stories. From our earliest days as thinking beings, we employed every available tool to tell each other stories. We danced, drew pictures on the walls of our caves, spoke, and sang. All of this extraordinary effort was designed to entertain, recount the news of the day, explain natural occurrences—and then gradually to build religious and cultural traditions and establish the common bonds and continuity that eventually formed civilizations. Stories are the most powerful force in the universe; they are the primary element that has distinguished our evolutionary path.

Our love of the story has not diminished with time. Enormous segments of societies are devoted to the art of storytelling. Book sales in the United States alone topped $24 billion in 2006; movie studios spend fortunes to create and promote stories; and the news industry is more pervasive in its presence than ever before.

There is no mystery to our fascination. Great stories are magic. They can introduce us to new cultures or remind us of the nobility and failures of our own; inspire us to greatness or scare us to death; but above all, stories provide human insight on a level that is unavailable through any other source. In fact, stories connect each of us to the rest of humanity not just in our own time, but also throughout history.

This special magic of books is the greatest treasure that we can hand down from generation to generation. In fact, that spark in a child that comes from books became the motivation for the creation of my organization, First Book, a national literacy program with a simple mission: to provide new books to the most disadvantaged children. First Book has been at work in hundreds of communities for over a decade. Every year, children in need receive millions of books through our organization, and millions more are provided through dedicated literacy institutions across the United States and around the world. In addition, groups of people dedicate themselves tirelessly to working with children to share reading and stories in every imaginable setting from schools to the streets. Of course, this Herculean effort serves many important goals. Literacy translates to productivity and employability in life and many other valid and even essential elements. But at the heart of this movement are people who love stories, love to read, and want desperately to ensure that no one misses the wonderful possibilities that reading provides.

When thinking about the importance of books, there is an overwhelming urge to cite the literary devotion of great minds. Some have written of the magnitude of the importance of literature. Amy Lowell, an American poet, captured the concept when she said, "Books are more than books. They are the life, the very heart and core of ages past, the reason why men lived and worked and died, the essence and quintessence of their lives." Others have spoken of their personal obsession with books, as in Thomas Jefferson's simple statement: "I live for books." But more compelling, perhaps, is the almost instinctive excitement in children for books and stories.

Throughout my years at First Book, I have heard truly extraordinary stories about the power of books in the lives of children. In one case, a homeless child, who had been bounced from one location to another, later resurfaced—and the only possession that he had fought to keep was the book he was given as part of a First Book distribution months earlier. More recently, I met a child who, upon receiving the book he wanted, flashed a big smile and said, "This is my big chance!" These snapshots reveal the true power of books and stories to give hope and change lives.

As these children grow up and continue to develop their love of reading, they will owe a profound debt to those volunteers who reached out to them—a debt that they may repay by reaching out to spark the next generation of readers. But there is a greater debt owed by all of us—a debt to the storytellers, the authors, who have bound us together, inspired our leaders, fueled our civilizations, and helped us put our children to sleep with their heads full of images and ideas.

WHO WROTE THAT? is a series of books dedicated to introducing us to a few of these incredible individuals. While we have almost always honored stories, we have not uniformly honored storytellers. In fact, some of the most important authors have toiled in complete obscurity throughout their lives or have been openly persecuted for the uncomfortable truths that they have laid before us. When confronted with the magnitude of their written work, we can forget that writers are people. They struggle through the same daily indignities and dental appointments, and they experience the intense joy and bottomless despair that many of us do. Yet, somehow they rise above it all to weave a powerful thread that connects us all. It is a rare honor to have the opportunity that these books provide to share the lives of these extraordinary people. Enjoy.

The winners of the 1999 Hispanic Heritage Awards included (left to right) Anthony Munoz for sports, Tina Ramirez for education, Placido Domingo for the arts, Antonia Hernandez for leadership, and Gary Soto for literature. Soto is a distinguished Mexican-American writer of adult and children's literature.

1

I Am Chicano

IN 1990, GARY Soto made publishing history. In that year, his first book for children, *Baseball in April and Other Stories*, was published by Harcourt Publishers. According to Soto, it was the first book written by a Mexican American, or "Chicano" as he prefers to be called, to be published by a major New York publishing house. (See "Did You Know..." on page 12 for a further discussion of the meaning of the word *Chicano*.)

It was a major breakthrough for Mexican Americans everywhere. As Rudolfo Anaya said in *World Literature Today*, "Entire generations of Mexican American schoolchildren went through elementary school without ever having read a story about their culture or communities."[1] Gary Soto changed that. Through his writing, for the first time, young Mexican Americans were able to see themselves in books. He has shown readers everywhere, whatever their heritage, the lives, hopes and dreams of Mexican Americans.

Although Soto's work is mainly set in Mexican-American communities, the themes are universal. His characters are usually of Mexican heritage, but anyone, Mexican American or not, can relate to them. His characters may sit down to a meal of frijoles and tortillas rather than a cheeseburger and fries, but their thoughts and emotions are understood by all.

Although Soto uses Spanish words and phrases throughout his texts (he includes a glossary at the back of each book to help non–Spanish speakers translate), he appeals to readers everywhere. As Diane Roback of *Publisher's Weekly* noted, "The conflicts and feelings expressed are universal."[2]

Did you know...

Gary Soto prefers the term *Chicano* because it describes Mexican Americans who have a strong sense of identity and an accompanying sense of political and social awareness. To Soto, being Chicano (or Chicana, if you're female) indicates that you're proud of being Mexican American!

As Soto himself said in a profile published in *Macmillan Profiles: Latino Americans*, "Even though I write a lot about life in the barrio, I am really writing about the lives and experiences of most American kids; having a pet, going to the park for a family cookout, running through a sprinkler on a hot day, and getting a bee sting!"[3]

How does he do it? How does Gary Soto make his stories of life in the barrio accessible and interesting to readers of all kinds?

First, he is enormously gifted in the use of imagery and specific details in telling a tale. This allows him to create and describe settings and situations that the reader can easily envision. The characters that he creates are well-drawn, honest, and realistic. These talents allow Soto to create a literary world that is interesting and welcoming to all. Because of this, Gary Soto is considered by many to be among the most important contemporary authors in the United States.

He is also one of the most prolific. His output as a writer is truly astonishing: Since the publication of his first book in 1977, a collection of poetry entitled *The Elements of San Joaquin*, he has published more than 40 titles. Unlike many writers, he has never been content with just writing one kind of book. He has always been interested in taking chances and exploring his capabilities both as an artist and a Chicano.

Among adult readers, Gary Soto is perhaps most famous as a poet. As Gerald Stern said in his blurb for Soto's *New and Selected Poems*, "I read Gary Soto's poems with delight. There's no one I know, certainly in this language, who writes like him. For me, his is a deeply important poetry."[4]

In addition to poetry, he also writes fiction for adults, including titles such as *Nickel and Dime*, which explores the lives of three different men and deals with poverty and loss of hope. He has also written a series of autobiographical essays that explore his life; these have been collected in books such as *Living Up the Street* and *The Effects of Knut Hamsun on a Fresno Boy*.

Since 1990, however, his greatest fame has been as a writer of books for children of all ages. He has written colorful picture books for young readers with titles such as *Too Many Tamales*, *Big Bushy Mustache,* and *Chato and the Party Animals*. He has written gritty, realistic novels for young adults including the books *Taking Sides* and *Buried Onions*. He has written poetry for young adults, including the collections *A Fire In My Hands: A Book of Poems*, *Canto Familiar*, and *Fearless Fernie: Hanging Out With Fernie and Me*.

He has written two plays: *Novio Boy: A Play* and *Nerdlandia*. He has written the libretto (or book) for the opera *Nerdlandia*, based on his play. He has even written and directed three movies, including the award-winning *The Pool Party*.

Because of his wide-ranging output, Gary Soto has done something that very few authors are able to achieve: He has created a literary world for all ages. As Susan Marie Swanson noted in a *Riverbank Review* profile of Gary Soto, "A child could grow up on Soto's books." A reader could start with the picture books, move on to the young adult novels, and finally graduate to the adult fiction and poetry. "How many American authors have mapped such a journey for us to follow?" Swanson wondered. "Soto's is an extraordinary achievement."[5]

Gary Soto (center) poses with his sister Debbie, his mother, Angie, and his brother Rick (right), in 1963. When Soto was a child, his family was quite poor. At some point all members of the family had to work to contribute to the household.

Throughout his career, critics have applauded Soto's work. From his poetry—"Gary Soto's poems are fast, funny, heartrending, and achingly believable, like Polaroid love letters, or snatches of music heard out of a passing car; patches of beauty like patches of sunlight; the very pulse of life"[6]—to his fiction—"[Soto writes] in bleak sentences of whispered beauty. A valuable tale, it's one that makes no concessions"[7]—to his essays—"One of those rare books that come from the author's heart, tempered by his intelligence and made alive by imaginative spirit"[8]—he has been acclaimed as one of America's best authors.

It is truly extraordinary that Gary Soto ever became a writer in the first place. He grew up in an older Chicano neighborhood of Fresno, California. His family was poor, and everyone in the family had to work hard just to keep a roof over their heads, food on the table, and clothes on their backs. In such a household, no one has time to read for fun, to write, or even to dream.

Young Soto had to contend not only with growing up poor; growing up in the barrio was difficult itself. Poverty can do bad things to people. Under such circumstances, crime, drugs, and violence are everyday occurrences. Escape from such a life seems impossible, and hope for a better future is rare. As he said in an interview in the literary journal *Ploughshares*, Soto felt that he would "marry Mexican poor, work Mexican hours, and in the end, die a Mexican death, broke and in despair."[9] For many, staying in school and avoiding prison was a major accomplishment.

It is easy to wonder, given his early life, just how Gary Soto managed to do it. How was he able to make a new life for himself? He grew up in a family in which nearly every member was a nonreader, so how did he discover the world of books and literature? How did he become the writer of whom Hector Torres said in the 1989 *Dictionary of Literary Biography*, "Soto's consistent attention to the craft of writing and his sensitivity to his subject matter have earned him an indisputable place in American and Chicano literature"?[10]

Nearly everyone who lived in Fresno, California, during the 1950s worked in agriculture. Today, agriculture is still an important industry in the area. Above, a farm worker dumps oranges in a bin after picking them in the orchard.

2

Barrio Boy

IN THE EARLY 1950s, Fresno, California, was a rough-and-tumble city of less than 100,000 inhabitants. Many of its citizens were what is known as "working poor." This meant that, despite the fact that many, if not everyone, in a family worked, they still could not earn enough money to live above the poverty level. These families were largely Mexican American, Asian American, African American, and what is commonly referred to as "Okie" (see "Did You Know..." on page 20).

Nearly everyone who worked in the region worked in agriculture. Some toiled in processing plants that sorted, boxed, and shipped the produce grown in the area. Others worked out in the fields. Every day, workers in the city would climb aboard ramshackle trucks and buses that would take them out to work on the farms of the surrounding San Joaquin Valley.

The work was tough, the hours were long, and the pay was inadequate, to say the least. To make ends meet, children would often have to quit school and work alongside their families in the fields. Without education, they were condemned to the same hard lives as their parents. Generation after generation, families worked the same dead-end jobs, struggling just to survive. Among these families were the Sotos.

Gary Soto's paternal grandfather, Francisco (Frank) Soto, had left Mexico as a young man and had finally settled in Fresno. Like many others, he left Mexico in search of a better life north of the border. What he found instead was years of backbreaking labor. He also found a wife.

Her name was Pola. When Frank Soto met her, she was selling ice cream cones on the street to support herself and

Did you know...

The term *Okie* originally referred to someone from the state of Oklahoma. During the days of the Dust Bowl in the 1930s, however, when large numbers of farmers migrated to California from the Great Plains and the Southwest in search of a better life, all migrant farm workers were referred to as "Okies." Historically, the word was used as an insult, but today many Okies use the term proudly, as a badge of honor and as a symbol of the Okie survivor attitude.

her child. She had given birth to the child when she was just a teenager in Mexico. Soon after, she immigrated to the United States, fleeing the political and social turmoil of the Mexican Revolution (1910–1920).

Frank and Pola soon fell in love, married, and began a family. They and their children worked from sunrise to sunset in the fields, picking oranges, grapes, plums, peaches, and even cotton. Pola soon left the fields to work in a fruit packaging factory. There, she worked on a conveyer belt that carried raisins. Her job was to sort through the raisins, picking out any leaves, twigs, or pebbles that may have been mixed in with the fruit.

Pola Soto retired while in her late fifties. Not only had she worked full-time most of her life, but she had also raised a family, including Gary's father, Manuel Soto.

Manuel Soto met Gary's mother, Angie Trevino, in 1947 at Edison High School in Fresno. Trevino had worked in the fields in Texas and Michigan before moving to Fresno. Soto and Trevino attended school whenever possible, but, like many others of their class, they were unable to finish their educations and left high school before graduating.

They married when they were just 18 and soon began to have children. Their oldest son, Rick, was born on June 28, 1950. Gary, the middle child, was born on April 12, 1952. Gary's younger sister, Debra, was born on March 6, 1953.

Gary's mother and father both had to work hard in order to support their growing family. Manuel Soto packed boxes at the Sun-Maid Raisin Company. Angie Soto peeled potatoes at the Redi-Spuds factory. They worked long hours but earned minimum wage. By the time they got home from work they were both exhausted, with little energy or desire to spend quality time with their children.

WHERE HE LIVED

The Soto family lived in South Fresno on Braly Street. Many other family members, including Gary's grandmother, lived close by. The family members often visited each other and helped each other when needed.

Their house was next to a junkyard that dealt in metals of all kinds. Down the street was the Sun-Maid Raisin Company. Not only did Gary's father and grandmother work there, so did three uncles, an aunt, and even a dog, which tagged along with Gary's grandfather while he was working as a security guard.

Also in the vicinity of Gary's house was Challenge Milk, a printing shop, and a 7-Up bottling company, where, Soto admitted, he and his brother stole sodas once or twice. Down the alley from the family house was a broom factory, and across from the broom factory lived the Molina family. The Molina kids and the Soto kids spent their summers playing together. With no playgrounds nearby, the kids spent their time playing in the streets, down the alleys, and at the Molina house.

As Gary later described in *Living Up the Street*, "There were eight children on the block . . . ranging from twelve down to one, so there was much to do: Wrestle, eat raw bacon, jump from the couch, sword fight with rolled-up newspapers, steal from neighbors, kick chickens, throw rocks at passing cars. . . ."[1]

In fact, Gary has said that jumping on the couch is one of the purest, happiest memories of his childhood. As he said in an interview, "I remember sort of sneaking around, our mom would go to visit relatives around the block, and then we'd wait for her to go away, and we'd get up on the couch and start jumping on it. It was me and Rick, and the Molina family kids."[2]

In **Living Up the Street,** *Soto described the children in his neighborhood: "There were eight children on the block . . . ranging from twelve down to one, so there was much to do. . . ." Above, young Gary (second from right, in striped shirt) gathers with some of his childhood friends.*

Growing up poor, there was no money available for luxuries like toys. Kids would have to make do with what they could. Gary's first toys were uncooked pinto beans and rocks that he used as toy soldiers.

Gary is convinced that this very absence of things helped to make him a writer. As he once pointed out, his neighborhood was blighted. There weren't many neighbors, just factories and vacant lots and a few families who eventually moved away. Gary is certain that he developed his powers of observation—his skills of watching, observing, and remembering—because his family had to make do with had so little.

PLAYING WITH FIRE

The family may have owned few possessions, but thanks to Gary and his siblings' attempts to play with fire, they once almost owned even fewer. As Soto described the incident in the chapter entitled "Being Mean" in *Living Up the Street*, it happened in the summer of 1957, when Gary was just five. Rick, Gary, and Debra had been at their grandmother's house watching the first television set that anyone in the family had owned. The show was about how to prevent fires.

The children were enthralled. When they returned home, they made houses out of shoeboxes, drawing windows, cutting out doors, and pretending that ants placed in the boxes were people. Then, they would set the shoeboxes on fire.

Soon enough, though, burning shoeboxes became boring. Rick suggested that they start a house fire. The three kids crumpled old newspapers and placed them in piles around the house. They then set them on fire and enjoyed watching the fire leap from newspaper pile to newspaper pile. Fortunately, the three were smart enough to have dragged the garden hose into the house. They spent hours starting fires and then putting them out. Soon, the walls were covered with ash and the floor was a soggy mess.

Even starting fires can get boring, though. The three started throwing cherry tomatoes at each other, making red splotches of tomato all over each other and the walls, until all the tomatoes were gone. Gary quickly fell asleep, exhausted from the day's fun. It was at that point that their mother, also exhausted from another long day of peeling potatoes, arrived home.

She was furious. As Gary remembered, he woke up to his mother yelling and spanking Rick. Knowing that he was going to be next, Gary fled the house to go play at the Molinas' house, staying away until his mother's temper had cooled.

One of Soto's earliest memories is of eating M&Ms and staring out his bedroom window at the junkyard next door. He also remembers being three, sitting in the dirt, and watching his mother in the field cutting grapes.

Gary spent a lot of time playing with his brother and sister. Rick was a typical bullying older brother. He was, as Soto remembers, "larger than me, he was tougher than me, and more worldly than me. The way he dressed was the way I would have to dress. He would just cue me in without telling me how I was supposed to be."[3]

It is unfortunate but true that brothers and sisters do not always grow up to be friends. In an interview, Gary described his sister Debra as a "pretty feisty girl." She was very quick to anger and got into a lot of fights. Rick and Gary are still friends, but, as Gary said in a phone interview, "My sister . . . I haven't seen her in sixteen years. If I did see her, I'd just go the other way. [There's a difference in our] priorities, in what people want from life. This goes back to her being quick to anger."[4]

Despite the squabbles, while they were growing up, all members of the family relied on each other to survive. Sometimes, there wasn't enough food. Meals were mostly frijoles (beans) that everyone would scoop up in the warm tortillas that Gary's mother prepared at every meal. Gary, though, didn't really care about food when he was growing up. As he said in a phone interview, "I think even when I was born, the first couple of months, my mom said I would hardly eat at all. In many ways, I was stunted, physically and even mentally. It was my own fixation—I wasn't like a kid who was just gobbling food. I was just really skinny."[5]

When Gary was four and a half, his mother and father separated for about six months. One day, Gary went to visit his father, who was staying with his Uncle Shorty. "I remember opening the refrigerator and there was nothing but a little puckered apple. I was thinking, 'well, geez,' and there was literally nothing to eat but water and that little puckered apple. And I remember just closing it . . . when you're a kid you do want to eat *something*!"[6]

After Gary's father and mother reconciled, his father moved back home. Life in the Soto family seemed to getting back to normal. Tragedy was about to strike the Soto family, though, a tragedy that would change everything.

TRAGEDY

One day in August 1957, Gary's father was at work when the unthinkable happened. A coworker and friend of the family, who lived just five houses down from the Sotos, was climbing a ladder with a tray of nails on his shoulder. The man lost his balance and fell on top of Gary's father, breaking his neck. Manuel Soto, age 27, died just two days later, leaving behind a widow with three young children to support. Gary's life and that of his family would never be the same.

Like any five-year-old, Gary was scared and confused by his father's death. He remembers his mother crying. He remembers his relatives crying and trying to console him. He remembers seeing his father inside the casket at the funeral. He does not remember ever crying himself: He had buried his own feelings deep inside.

Because Gary was very young when Manuel Soto died, he has few clear memories of his father. He does remember a strong image of him painting the side of the family house. Even then, Gary knew that it was hard work and that his father was trying to build a better life for his family.

Although Manuel Soto tried to do his best for his family, according to Gary, he had a hard time expressing his feelings. As Soto said in a phone interview, "He was a moody man, brooding. Very quiet. I don't remember him ever picking me up, or doing the fatherly kind of things. My memory is not unkind, but I think he was remote."[7]

Soon after his father's death, Gary and his family moved away from South Fresno and settled in a rough neighborhood in an industrial area of Fresno. Moving to a new home seemed to close the book on Manuel Soto's death. Despite the loss, the family didn't talk about him again.

Gary Soto remembered this in the essay "This Man" from his marvelous essay collection *The Effects of Knut Hamsun on a Fresno Boy*: "Something happened to our family without us being aware, a quiet between mother and children settled on us like dust. We went to school, ate, watched television that wasn't funny, and because mother never said anything, father, too, became that name we never said in our house."[8]

The man who accidentally caused Manuel Soto's death never came to visit the family, even to apologize. In the essay "This Man," written many years after his father's death, Soto speculated on the man's life. He hopes that the man has not forgotten what he did; remembers what he did, even if it was an accident; and knows about the pain that he caused. As Soto said in the essay, "We lived poor years because he died. We suffered quietly and hurt even today. Shouldn't this mean anything to him?"[9]

For the two years after his father's death, Gary was raised by his mother and grandparents. All of the adults in the family were forced to work hard, taking whatever jobs they could find to help support Angie Soto and her three growing kids. Still, money was scarce. Life was hard, and the future did not look a whole lot brighter.

Above is Soto's high school identification card. Though he struggled in school, in high school he discovered wrestling, rock music, and literature, all of which would help him learn more about himself.

3

Growing Up Poor

GROWING UP POOR is difficult for any child. There is never enough to eat, never new clothes to wear, never any money around for anything but the basic necessities of life. Growing up in a single-parent household is difficult as well. One parent, working full-time, comes home exhausted at the end of the day and can find it difficult to provide the care and attention that growing children require. These were the basic conditions of Gary Soto's early childhood.

Added to that, Gary was Mexican American. It is easy to forget, from today's perspective, how much things have changed during the past 50 years. Today, Mexican-American, and indeed, all Latino or Hispanic cultures, have become part of the American culture. Musicians such as Ricky Martin, Shakira, and Juanes; actors such as Salma Hayek and George Lopez; and writers such as Pablo Neruda, Laura Esquivel, Octavio Paz, and, yes, Gary Soto, are respected and popular artists among Americans of every national origin. Mexican food has become as popular—as "American"—as hamburgers or pizza. Today, more salsa is sold in the United States than ketchup.

When Gary was growing up, though, things were different. Prejudice against Mexican Americans was still strong. Their rights to vote, to earn a good wage, and to be treated fairly by the police was often infringed on. In some parts of the country, they were not allowed to serve on juries, and, with very few exceptions, they were all but invisible in the media.

Growing up, Gary rarely got to see people on television who looked like him, thought like him, or had a life like his. Popular television shows such as *Leave It to Beaver* showed middle-class white families in which the father went to work during the day; the wife stayed home to clean and cook; and the kids went to school, came home, and did their homework. To Gary, it was like watching a world he would never know or be a part of, a world completely unlike his own. As he wrote in the essay "Looking for Work," in his book *Living Up the Street*:

> I spent the mornings in front of the television that showed the comfortable lives of white kids. There were no beatings, no rifts in the family. They wore bright clothes; toys tumbled from their closets. They hopped into bed with kisses and woke to glasses of fresh orange juice, and to a father sitting before

> his morning coffee while the mother buttered his toast. They hurried through the day making friends and gobs of money, hurrying home to a warmly lit living room, and then dinner (*Living Up the Street*, p. 30)

These factors made growing up difficult for Gary. He brooded over the loss of his father and hated the fact that, because of his family's poverty, he could not wear the same clothes as the "cool" kids. He was also, as he said, "very much aware that he [was] Mexican American and that there [was] a division among races. [He was also] aware that Mexican Americans suffer."[1]

As he said in an interview with *Scholastic*,

> Growing up in Fresno, there was some racism—probably a lot. There was a feeling of being second-rate compared to everybody else. It affects your self-esteem, what you feel you can do, and your career path. It may make you angry, or it may make you defeated at a very early age. . . . It does affect your personality.[2]

Nothing that Gary Soto had seen in his life gave him hope that things could or would change. His life, like that of his parents and that of their parents, was all but laid out for him. A lifetime of poverty, early marriage, and the never-ending possibility of violence seemed to be his destiny. As he said in an interview in the literary journal *Ploughshares,* "The likelihood of going beyond that was miniscule." Unfortunately, the next few years would not offer him any possibility of escape.[3]

FAILING IN SCHOOL

During his first years of school—kindergarten and first grade—Gary attended three different schools: Emerson

Elementary, Webster Elementary, and Winchell Elementary. Moving from school to school made it difficult for Gary to make friends, as well as to keep up with his classes. He was quickly labeled a poor student.

As he said in a phone interview, "I was terrible in school. My brother flunked first grade, and I thought, Who flunks first grade? But then, I almost flunked first grade myself! I think it might have been the environment in the house, the lack of nutrition. I don't know exactly why."[4]

It could, in fact, have been any combination of those factors. Studies show that, when children do not get enough to eat, they can find it difficult to concentrate and do well in school. When Gary attended school, he did not receive the free breakfast and lunch that schools are now required to provide to those who need assistance. Imagine trying to learn at school if your stomach was constantly growling.

Gary's home environment was definitely a factor in his failure to do well in school. He grew up in a home in which there were no books, and he got no real encouragement to study and do better. Gary admitted in an interview, "I think that could have been a part of my poor study habits. I don't think that my parents really cared about education. I don't think. . . . I don't remember them ever taking us to the library. They were busy doing chores around the house."[5]

Certainly, nothing in his family or educational background gave any hint that he would become a writer. As he mentioned in an interview with *Contemporary Authors*, "I don't think I had any literary aspirations when I was a kid. In fact we were pretty much an illiterate family. We didn't have books, and no one encouraged us to read. So my wanting to write poetry was pretty much a fluke."[6]

Gary's mother did care about his education to a certain extent. In an effort to help him do better in school, she somehow found the money to put him in St. John's Elementary School, a private Catholic school. He attended St. John's from second to fourth grade.

The experiment did not work. In the essay "Deceit" in *Living Up the Street*, Soto described his time at St. John's as a time when "short nuns threw chalk at me, chased me with books cocked over their heads, squeezed me into cloak closets and, on slow days, asked me to pop erasers and to wipe the blackboard clean."[7]

In another interview, Soto remembered, "The Catholic School had ways of making me feel bad . . . like putting me in wastebaskets, or making you stand with your nose against the wall if you were caught chewing gum."[8] For Gary, St. John's was a place of continuous petty humiliations.

In 1963, Gary moved from St. John's back to Jefferson Elementary School, a public school. St. John's was too far from their house, and his mother could no longer afford the tuition of the private school.

In 1963–1964, for fifth and sixth grades, Gary attended Jefferson Elementary School. There, his grades briefly improved. One teacher, Mr. Basmajian, was his favorite; he struck Gary as being tough but helpful. As Soto said in a phone interview, "He was a man who was very fair, who seemed to care about us. I really wanted to live up to his expectations. I hadn't gotten that before."[9]

This is not to say that Gary was a great student—his favorite classes were singing, art, and physical education. It was obvious, though, that, with a little encouragement and a teacher that expected him to do well, he *could* do well.

Even with a good teacher, however, school could still be a humiliating experience for Gary and other students like him. As he recalled in a phone interview:

> I remember we had two rows, actually three rows, two rows were dedicated to the "dumb" students, that's how they were labeled. And then the third one was for the smart kids. I was always the leader of the dumb kids. Sometimes I'd make it up into the other category, but I'd always end up being sent back to the other row. It was like I was always on the verge. And that's what the system was, not to hold it against Mr. Basmajian.[10]

Another event that had a major impact on Gary's life took place in 1963: His mother remarried. Gary's new stepfather was James Oftedal. He worked in a warehouse at a book distribution center. Not only did Gary have to adjust to life with a new father, but there were also two new mouths to feed: Gary's younger stepbrothers, James and Martin. Gary has remained friends with both of his stepbrothers. As he described them in an interview,

> My stepbrothers are good guys. They're fine. They're very affectionate to my mother. I do like both of them . . . James, for example, works for the U.S. Forest Service and he is involved in a program that gets kids involved in forestry. I like that aspect of his life because I want all kids to do well.[11]

The pressure of having to support five kids weighed heavily on Gary's stepfather. He toiled long, exhausting hours lifting heavy boxes of books on a conveyer belt to feed, clothe, and house his family. He also drank heavily. He would often stop at a local bar for a few drinks before coming home, where he would drink more. He would then spend the rest of the evening sitting in his easy chair, the arms of which, as Soto described, were "slick from wear and oily forearms,"[12] staring blankly at the television set.

NO WAY OUT

Moving on to Washington Junior High School, Gary's grades began a slow decline. One bright spot was his time in the Cadet program, which was a military club. He joined partly in the hope that the program would help give him a sense of discipline and responsibility. The main reason he joined, though, was that he thought that the uniforms, covered with the ribbons he hoped to earn, would help him get a girlfriend. He described it in a phone interview:

> It was like looking sharp. I had a rank. I really was into that. The whole school was into it. There were between 200 and 250 cadets out of 1500 students. Everybody was a cadet. There was the rifle, and you could carry a rifle, and wear a uniform, it was just really sharp. What happened was they gave you this old G.I. uniform, meant for grown men. But men are men, and they have different bodies than kids, so I went out to buy my own khaki pants. It was good.[13]

Soto described his original uniform in the chapter entitled "Desire" in his book of nonfiction, *Living Up the Street*, "On Fridays I wore my uniform that was clearly meant for an adult. My pant legs billowing in the slightest wind; the shirt pockets came down below my ribs almost to my belly button."[14] Obviously this was not a look that would attract the "cool" girls that Gary was attracted to.

His parents had no money to buy him new clothes, though, even just one new pair of khakis. In Gary's mind, he would never be able to get a girlfriend without wearing the proper clothes. For that to happen, he would have to earn the money himself.

Gary had always had odd jobs. He had gone door to door in the neighborhood, offering to rake leaves and pull weeds from flower beds. He had collected cans and bottles and had a morning newspaper delivery route. He had even gone out with his Uncle Shorty, a veteran of the Korean War, looking for copper wire to collect.

That summer, when he was 14, he went out with his mother to work in the fields for the first time. They would get up at dawn to eat a quick breakfast before driving out to the vineyards. There, armed with a grape knife and a pan to collect the grapes, they would go up and down the rows, bent over, cutting the ripe bunches of grapes. Every two pans collected would equal one larger tray. For each tray, they would receive six cents. On his first day of work, by lunchtime, he had picked 37 trays of grapes—worth about $2.50. His mother had earned more than four times that.

So it went, day after day, for the entire 13 days it took to pick the harvest. At the end of that time, Gary had earned only $53. His mother had earned about $300 for two weeks of hot, backbreaking labor. With his earnings, Gary was able to buy a pair of khakis, two shirts, and a stylish maroon colored T-shirt.

Gary gained more than that, though. Prior to this experience, his only knowledge of his mother's difficult work was her exhaustion when she came from the fields. Now, he had firsthand knowledge of how hard farm workers had to toil for so little money. It made him determined never to have to work like that if he could help it.

The problem was not just that nobody expected more from him because he was Mexican American and poor. The truth was, Gary did not expect much from himself.

When Gary was 14, he went into the fields to work with his mother for the first time. Though this took place in the 1960s, children today still help their families by working. The girl above, Ana Alvaros, was 10 years old when this picture was taken in 1997.

As he said in a phone interview, "I think [in part because of] the commercial world and television world (shows like "Leave It to Beaver") made me feel like a second class citizen. I think racially, that's how we felt. Lots of Mexican kids didn't feel like we were going to make it."[15]

Imagine growing up and never seeing people who looked like you doing any kind of work but hard physical labor. Imagine growing up and watching television and never seeing anyone on the screen that looked like you at all! It would be difficult, if not impossible, to grow up feeling good about yourself, to believe that you were, indeed, anything more than a second-class citizen.

Even his parents could not envision a better life for their son. As Soto said in a phone interview, "I think they thought I was going to work in a warehouse, or delivering something, or cooking, or . . . whatever people do . . . but not agricultural, they knew that wasn't going to happen. [They knew] I wasn't going to do that no more."[16]

This goes a long way in explaining why, even from the time of kindergarten, Soto grew up feeling what he described as a "sense of doom."[17] He grew up thinking that the cards were stacked against him, that, because of his birth and social status, he never stood a chance.

You might wonder how someone as young as five years old can have a sense of doom, but as Soto described it in a phone interview:

> I already knew that it would take intelligence and money to get by in life. I think kids at an early age understand that there's something larger looming outside just playing. . . . I already felt like I didn't think I would make it. Whatever that meant. I looked at the world around me, factories: the pickle factory, the broom factory, diesels going up and down the block, and I knew it wasn't right. I had a sense that things weren't going to work out. I did have some joy, playing, just playing, but I didn't think I was going to make it.[18]

For a while, it did not look like he was going to make it. Going from junior high school to Roosevelt High did not improve things. As Soto phrased it, his grades "sputtered."[19] He also liked girls but found it difficult to get a girlfriend.

Going to high school did have one plus side. According to Gary, "Junior high was really violent, there were lots of fights. I was involved, but not a whole lot . . . it was a scary scene. I thought high school was going to be like that. But it was pastoral. People were much more mature."[18]

In high school, Gary discovered wrestling. He wrestled all three years (tenth through twelfth grade) of high school in the 95- and 103-pound weight classes. He admits, though, that he was not very good.

This was also the time that Gary discovered rock music. As some people feel, this is the time when rock music was at its best. Gary and his best friend, Scott, listened to artists such as the Beatles, the Animals, Donovan, and Bob Dylan. Gary's favorite group was the Rolling Stones. He loved their bluesy sound. The fact that they were also his brother's favorite group didn't hurt either.

In high school, Gary also began to discover the joys of literature. Some of his early favorites were books by American literary giants Ernest Hemingway (1899–1961) and John Steinbeck (1902–1968). He especially enjoyed *The Old Man and the Sea* by Hemingway and *The Grapes of Wrath* and *In Dubious Battle* by Steinbeck. These books, as well as others by these authors, are still read by students and readers around the world. But the book that had the greatest influence on Gary during his high school years is rarely read today.

Gary first read *To Sir, With Love* by E.R. Braithwaite, when he was in eleventh grade. Today, the book is largely remembered for inspiring a movie version starring Sidney Poitier, as well as the hit title song, sung by the 1960s star Lulu. Before it was a movie, before it was a song, it was a best-selling novel.

The book is largely autobiographical, based on Braithwaite's personal experiences. It tells the story of Ricardo Braithwaite, a British–West Indian-born communications engineer. Living in London, he is unable to find work in his profession because of racism (Braithwaite is black) and becomes a teacher at a tough school in London's East End. After a rough beginning, he earns the trust and confidence of his students and realizes his love of teaching. (The real-life E.R. Braithwaite went on to write more books and become involved in social work. He even became the country of Guyana's permanent representative to the United Nations.)

Gary was enthralled by the book. Although it took place in London, he could see himself as one of the students in a school in a poor neighborhood where kids had little hope of a better life. Other aspects of the book appealed as well. As he said in a phone interview, "*To Sir, With Love* was a great literary read for me. I liked the aspect where you had a black teacher who took care of his kids and cared about them."[21]

Although books were becoming a form of solace and he enjoyed wrestling and hanging out with Scott, this was still a difficult period in Gary's life. School wasn't going well, and his grades showed it. Sadly, he still had not learned the study skills necessary to do well and get good grades.

His home life was going badly as well. There was constant fighting with both his mother and his stepfather—

Did you know...

Although Gary Soto enjoyed reading Hemingway and Steinbeck while he was in high school, today, his favorite classic author is John Galsworthy! John Galsworthy (1867–1933), who won the Nobel Prize for Literature in 1932, is best known for his series of novels known collectively as *The Forsyte Saga*. Soto admires Galsworthy's ability to write about English social classes in a witty, enlightening, and accurate manner.

sometimes just arguments, sometimes actual physical fights. Gary described this period as the time when his relationship with his parents soured, and stayed sour for years. Things got so bad that, during the summer of 1969, between his junior and senior years of high school, Gary ran away from home.

ESCAPE

With no money and nowhere to go, Gary resorted to hitching rides and living on the street. He slept wherever he could: on people's lawns, in parked cars, and even in the balcony of a church. Food was whatever he could find and wherever he could find it—sometimes just a package of crackers. He would wash up in gas station restrooms and fill empty soda bottles with water, corking them with scraps of paper.

Imagine living like that, and imagine how bad life must have been that living on the street was better than living at home. As Soto said in an interview with *The Pedestal* magazine, "It was a chilling scene at home. Why else would I run away when I was seventeen? Why would I have lived on the streets instead of in a home where everyday we were playing out 'Silence of the Lambs?' "[22]

Soto described his feelings at the time in the piece entitled "Black Hair" from his collection *Living Up the Street.*

> I started walking again, first up a commercial street, then into a residential area where I lay down on someone's lawn and replayed a scene at home—my mother crying at the kitchen table, my stepfather yelling with food in his mouth. They're cruel, I thought, and warned myself that I should never forgive them. How could they do this to me.[23]

Gary ended up in Glendale, California, nearly 200 miles from home. There, he found work at the Valley Tire Company. He worked eight hours a day loading tires, unloading tires, and moving tires from one place to another. At the end of the day, he was filthy, sweaty, and exhausted.

Although he had a job, he was not able to afford a place to live for another week. During that time, he was still living in parked cars or anywhere else he could find a place to spend the night. Finally, though, he was able to save up enough money to rent a room. His first night there was literally his first night's sleep in a real bed in more than two weeks.

Gary hated working at the Valley Tire Company. He had worked summers picking grapes and chopping cotton, so he knew what it was to work hard. Working at the Valley Tire Company, however, was even worse than working in the fields.

What deeply affected him were the lives of the other workers. Many of them were unskilled, some of them were undocumented (meaning they did not have the paperwork to allow them to work in the country legally), all of them were at the end of the road. Many of them had worked there for 12 years, and some even had sons working alongside them. It was a way of living, and an end to any sense of possibility, that Gary became desperate to avoid.

After seven weeks away, Gary returned home to begin his senior year in high school. On his arrival, he was concerned about how his parents would react, both to his running away and to his homecoming. His worry was not needed. As he described in a phone interview, "My stepfather kind of looked at me from the chair and then looked back at the television. I remember that very strongly. My mother was much more emotional."[24]

Gary returned to Roosevelt High for his senior year. One bright spot during that time was that he began to write poetry, though it was strictly for himself at first. Actually becoming a poet did not seem to be a possibility.

Gary's grades, on the other hand, still did not improve. He graduated from high school with only a 1.6 grade point average (GPA), the equivalent of a D+. Although graduating from high school was a major accomplishment, his GPA left him in a bit of trouble.

In 1969, the year that Gary graduated, the United States was still deeply involved in the Vietnam War and the draft was still in effect. Gary knew that if he did not go to college, it was very likely that he would be drafted and sent to Vietnam to fight in a war in which he did not believe. If he went to college, he would be eligible for a student deferment. For as long as he was in school and kept his grades up, he could not be drafted.

It was more than that, though. Gary knew what would happen to him if he did not earn a college degree. He knew that without it, he would end up either working in the fields like his parents or trapped in a minimum wage job like the guys at the Valley Tire Company.

Gary also knew that attending California State University at Fresno, his first choice of schools, was out of the question: His grades were just too low. Desperate to avoid either the draft or a dead-end job, Gary enrolled at Fresno City College, one of the few schools that would accept him with his low GPA. Fresno City College did have one thing in its favor: His brother Rick was already a student there. They would be able to get an apartment together, allowing Gary to get away from his home situation.

Gary was eager to move away from his parents and scared and excited about starting college. He had begun to appreciate the importance of education and had high hopes that college would allow him to get the education he felt that he had missed in public school. There was one more thing: He knew very well that Fresno City College could be his last chance at a better life.

When Gary graduated from high school, he knew that he had to pursue a college education in order to improve his life. Although he was not able to attend California State University at Fresno (pictured above) straight out of high school, he worked hard at Fresno City College and was able to transfer to the state university as a junior.

4

Discovering Himself Through Words

ONCE ACCEPTED INTO college, Gary Soto had another problem to face. What subject should he select as his major? He had gone through high school with no particular career in mind, but being in college demanded that he select a subject in which to specialize. What would it be? After much consideration, he finally settled on a major: geography!

Why would Soto decide to major in geography, with the idea of becoming a geographer? He said in an interview quoted on bookrags.com, that he chose geography "for no articulate reason except that I liked maps. I like seeing the world in print."[1]

There were other reasons as well. He thought that it might be the easiest choice of major. As he said in an interview with the literary journal *Ploughshares*, "I figured I'd just look at some maps, study some rivers, take multiple-choice tests, and that'd be that. Being semi-literate, I didn't want to get forced to write anything."[2] Imagine being a high school graduate and still considering yourself semi-literate.

Although geography was his major, Soto found himself spending more and more time in the library, educating himself by reading independently. He would read whatever he came across, picking up any book that looked interesting. He did this all though his first year of college, gradually expanding his knowledge of literature. As much as Soto enjoyed it, the reading was random. He was still searching and not finding exactly what he was looking for.

One day in his second year of college, when he was just 19, he came across a book that would change his life. He explained in *Contemporary Authors*, "I know the day the change began, because it was when I discovered in the library a collection of poems edited by Donald Allen. . . . I discovered this poetry and thought, This is terrific: I'd like to do something like this."[3] Studying geography would soon become a distant memory.

CROSSROADS

The book was called *The New American Poetry*. It was an anthology, a collection of what was considered to be the best new poetry written between 1945 and 1960. The poets in the collection, including Allen Ginsberg, John Ashbery, Denise Levertov, LeRoi Jones, Frank O'Hara, and Charles Olson, were once considered poetic revolutionaries—very different in style and subject from poets of previous generations. Of course, many of these poets, once thought to be odd, are today considered modern masters, part of the permanent canon of classic American literature.

Soto was blown away by the poetry. Like many others, he had never read poems like these before. This poetry spoke directly to Soto and talked about things that were relevant to his life. Before reading the collection, Soto had thought (as many people still do) that "poetry had to be about mountains, and streams and birds and stuff," as he mentioned in an interview with *Quill*.[4]

One poet in particular struck a chord with Soto. His name was Edward Field (1924–). Edward Field was not as well known as some of the other poets in the collection. He was a native New Yorker who wrote about subjects like trash, smog, and himself. As Soto also said to *Quill*, "Field wrote in a voice that was real common and I didn't know poetry could be like that."[5]

The poem that most influenced Soto was a poem by Field called "Unwanted." The poem is about a desperately lonely man, a man who has gone unnoticed all his life and feels alienated from society, alone, and unwanted. Is there anyone who has not felt like that way at one time or another?

Soto was no exception. When he read the poem, he realized that his feelings of alienation were not unique, that it was, as he said in an unpublished interview in 1988, "a human pain."[6]

In "Unwanted," Gary could see the power of poetry to take one person's experiences and make them universal. With one book, with one poem, he had found his vocation, his true self. As he said in an interview with *Ploughshares*, "I thought, Wow, wow, wow. I wanted to do this thing."[7]

A MAN WITH A MISSION

For the first time in his life, Soto saw his future clearly. He knew that he wanted to be a poet—that he had to be a poet. He also knew that it was a gamble, that very few people who dream of becoming poets are able to make a living do it. For Soto, the risk was worth it. Even if it meant being poor, he knew that it was what he had to give it a try.

Once the decision was made, there was no looking back, no regrets. As he said in a phone interview, "I had no doubts once I made the decision to become a poet. I knew what I wanted to do. I remember thinking that if I could do one little chapbook like twelve poems in a book, that I would be so happy. And then the dreams got larger and larger."[8]

Soto's grades had improved at Fresno City College, and in the fall of 1972, along with his brother, he transferred to California State University at Fresno. There, he changed his major from geography to English. He and his brother still lived together, along with Soto's best friend, Scott. After his father's death, Soto received a monthly social security payment of $92 per month, and that, along with money earned by gardening and working in a carwash, kept him going.

Did you know...

A chapbook, once referred to as a pamphlet, was formerly sold in Europe and America by itinerant agents known as chapmen. Chapbooks were, and still are, an inexpensive way to reach the reading public.

Poet Philip Levine is pictured above in 2006. While at Fresno, Gary Soto was able to take classes with Levine, during which he first began to grow as a poet.

At this stage of his life, though, Soto lived for literature. He read every poem he could lay his hands on. Poets such as Pablo Neruda, Charles Simic, and W. S. Merwin were among his favorites. They, along with many others, greatly influenced the poet that he was to become.

He was in the first stages of becoming a poet. While at California State University at Fresno, Soto took classes with the famous poet Philip Levine (1928–). Levine, who won the Pulitzer Prize for poetry in 1995, is famous for poetry that features animals and people of the working class. Some of his best-known poems are "They Feed the Lion" and "Animals Are Passing From Our Lives."

Levine's contribution to Soto's education was immense. He not only taught Soto how to take apart and analyze poems, he also taught him the nuts and bolts—the basic rules of writing poetry. Under his tutelage, Soto began to grow as a poet.

He gradually became more confident in his own abilities. One of his poems confirmed to him that he had made the right decision. "There was a little poem, kind of a silly poem, called 'Little League Tryouts,' about kids going out for Little League. It was a good experience for me just writing that poem, because I could tell a story about kids and baseball. And it had to do with failure, like those of Edward Field."[9] That poem later became the basis of the essay "Baseball in April" and then, even later, the short story of the same name.

Soto's growing confidence in his abilities coincided with outside events that encouraged him to follow his dream. The year 1973 saw major strikes by the United Farm Workers in the fields around Fresno, the same fields that Soto and his family had occasionally worked. Led by César Chávez, the strikers refused to work until their demands for better wages and working conditions were met.

César Chávez became a lifelong hero of Soto's. Soto loved the man and respected his lifelong devotion to the rights of farm workers. César Chávez's slogan, "Si, se

While Soto was in college, César Chávez began leading strikes by farm workers against the poor conditions in which they worked. Chávez was a great influence on Soto, who took to heart Chávez's slogan, "Si, se puede/Yes, you can."

puede/Yes, you can," helped give Soto the courage to follow his dream of becoming a writer.

Soto relished his time at California State University at Fresno. There, he was able to meet and become friends with other young aspiring poets. They become known as the Fresno School of Poets.

Soto graduated magna cum laude ("with distinction") with a bachelor of arts in English in 1974. (Rick Soto graduated in the same year and later became a successful graphic artist.) Two years later, in 1976, Soto received his master of fine arts degree in creative writing from the University of California at Irvine.

Unlike many of his fellow students, at the time of his graduation, he was already a published author. Soto had already begun the process of sending his poems to different magazines in the hope that they might be published. In spring of 1974, the *Iowa Review*, one of the country's most respected literary magazines, selected his nature poem "Kings Canyon/Earth" for publication. For a young, previously unpublished author, it was a great honor. You can imagine how excited Soto must have been. His dream of becoming a published poet had become a reality.

Not only was his poetry beginning to receive recognition, Soto was also in love. The relationship started in 1973, when he was 20 years old and he and his brother were, as Soto described it, "college poor." They were basically living off of whatever food they could take from their mother's refrigerator. One day, with a paycheck from Zak's Car Wash burning a hole in his pocket, Soto scrounged up 15 cents (one dime and five pennies) to buy a quart of beer to split with his brother. Then it happened.

He described it in his essay "Finding a Wife": "While I was returning home, swinging the quart of beer like a lantern, I saw the Japanese woman who was my neighbor, cracking walnuts on her front porch. I walked slowly so that she looked up, smiling. I smiled, said hello, and continued walking to the rhythm of her hammer rising and falling."[10]

They did not start dating immediately. Soto was still shy with girls and did not know how to approach her or what to say if he did. For weeks, he walked past her house, hoping to see her or even hid behind a hedge and waited until she came outside to water a plant or sweep the porch before walking past and nodding hello. Soon, they began to talk. Later, they would sit together on the porch eating sandwiches "as thick as Bibles," along with milk and "baked sweet bread flecked with tiny crushed walnuts."[11]

Her name was Carolyn Oda. She was the daughter of Japanese-American farm workers and had spent nine years working in the fields. She and Soto soon fell in love. Soto says that she is his "mate for life."[12] They married on May 24, 1975.

As Soto pointed out in the essay "Finding a Wife," it was fate that brought him and his wife together. "It was a chance meeting: I was walking past when she looked up to smile. It could have been somebody else, a girl drying persimmons on a line, or one hosing down her car, and I might have married another and been unhappy. But it was Carolyn, daughter of hard workers whom I found cracking walnuts."[13]

Soto's life had changed radically since he entered Fresno City College in 1970 feeling undereducated and uncertain about his future. Just six years later, he left school armed with a master's degree in creative writing. His poems were beginning to be recognized and published. Perhaps most important, he had met and married the love of his life. He was now ready to go out in the world and establish himself as a poet to be reckoned with.

Gary Soto poses with his wife, Carolyn (center), and daughter Mariko (left) in June 1999. As Soto's most trusted reader, his wife is asked almost daily to read Soto's latest "masterpiece."

5

Early Success

WRITING IS SOLITARY business. Unlike most other workers, a writer is basically alone with just his intelligence, imagination, and a pen and paper, typewriter, or computer, depending on the equipment of choice. As anyone who has written knows, it is hard to be totally objective about one's own writing. Because of this, most writers have people they trust read what they have written and give their honest opinions. Soto's most trusted reader is and always has been his wife.

As he says on his Web site, she is his first reader: "Poor thing, I bother her almost daily as I beg, 'Carolyn, could you please look at this masterpiece?' Of course, it's not a masterpiece, but a way of getting her attention."[1]

They quickly developed a system. He would give her a poem to read, and if she liked it, she would nod. Soto described it in his interview with *Ploughshares*:

> I would be working on a book of poems, and I'd say to her, "Do you like this?" and she would nod her head. I would decide, more or less, which poems to save by how many nods she gave me. But I'd be so nervous, waiting for her reaction, I'd think, Oh my God, maybe I'm a fraud, maybe this woman's going to call the Bureau of Consumer Fraud on me. I have to keep reminding myself that after all these books over all these years, I must be doing something right.[2]

That interview was conducted in spring of 1995, when Soto was already a well-established author. Even when he was starting out, though, he relied on his wife for the feedback and encouragement that he needed as a writer—and he did need encouragement, because, as with most beginning writers, success came slowly.

Some of his individual poems had been published in magazines such as *Poetry*. His talent was also being recognized early on with a series of awards. In 1975, he won an Academy of American Poets Prize as well as the Discovery/Nation Award. The United States Award of the International Poetry Forum and the University of California at Irvine's Chicano Contest Literary Prize were awarded to him in 1976. He received the Bess Hokin Prize from *Poetry* magazine in 1978.

BREAKTHROUGH

Soto had been able to get an individual poem published here and there, but getting a book publisher to issue a collection of his poems was another matter entirely. It is difficult for an unknown writer to find a publisher. It is even more difficult for an unknown poet to find a publisher. Books of poetry are rarely bestsellers, so a publisher must have a great deal of faith in a poet (as well as a love of his or her poems) to take a chance on publishing his or her book. With so many poets waiting to be discovered, what were the odds that it would happen for Soto? At times, it seemed like it might never happen.

As he recalled in a phone interview, "It was a miracle that my first book got published. I'd send stuff out to all the magazines, journals. . . . I wanted to be part of this literary world. Me and my friends would sit around at night, drink beer, talk about getting published, and complain about getting rejected."[3]

Then, the miracle happened. "My first book. I'd won a literary contest in 1976. There were a lot of literary contests, and I won one sponsored by the University of Pittsburgh Press. I won a prize, getting my book published. That was the turning point. I got $2,000.00, a trip to Pittsburgh, and a lot of notoriety."[4]

Soto's first poetry collection, entitled *The Elements of San Joaquin*, was published by the University of Pittsburgh Press in 1977. It was an astonishing personal achievement for Soto. The book's publication proved to Soto that it was, indeed, possible for him to escape the life of hard physical labor that he had dreaded, as well as the sense of doom that he had carried around with him since early childhood.

The poems in *The Elements of San Joaquin* offer a portrait of Mexican-American life. Soto's poems depict the life that he knew all too well: a life of violence in the city and backbreaking labor in the fields, coupled with a desire to return to a more innocent time of childhood. Soto received praise for his vivid descriptions of life as he knew it.

In the book *Chicano Poetry*, Juan Bruce-Novoa wrote that Soto's book "convinces because of its well-wrought structure, the craft, and the coherence of its totality." Bruce-Novoa also said that, because the collection brought such a full and realistic portrait of poverty to a reading public that was unfamiliar with that aspect of Mexican-American life, *San Joaquin* was "a social as well as a literary achievement."[5] This collection earned Soto the prestigious United States Award from the International Poetry Forum.

Soto himself believes that his collection was a breakthrough in Chicano literature. He says that, although previous poems spoke in general terms, *San Joaquin* spoke about a specific place (Fresno) when describing race. Soto helped put Fresno on the literary map.

Soto was thrilled to be published, but other members of his family did not know quite what to make of it. In the chapter entitled "Who Is Your Reader?" in the book *The Effects of Knut Hamsun on a Fresno Boy*, he describes going to his grandmother's house to present her with a copy of his book. Although she did not know how to read, she knew that it was a momentous occasion. She prepared a great meal for Soto—eggs, beans, and tortillas—and then put the book, completely unread, in a picture frame and placed it proudly on her coffee table.

Soto's work was earning him recognition, but it was not earning him much money. Even the best poets in the country find it hard to earn a living from their writing alone. Most find it necessary to teach in order to make ends meet. Gary Soto was no exception. In 1977, he began teaching Chicano studies at the University of California at Berkeley. He eventually became an associate professor in both the English and Chicano studies departments.

Soto would soon need the extra money. On July 21, 1978, he and his wife became parents. With the birth of their daughter, Mariko, Soto again experienced great change in his life. He was now a father, with another living being dependent on him for everything. Soto was thrilled but terrified to be a father. He still carried the memories of his own childhood, and he was determined to be the best father he could be for his daughter. He knew that raising her was, in some ways, another job that had to be done.

He discussed this in the chapter entitled "Getting It Done" in his autobiographical collection *The Effects of Knut Hamsun on a Fresno Boy*:

> This was particularly urgent because my own father died when I was six, leaving a hole in my soul no bigger than a pinprick. . . . I feared this mortal absence for my daughter, that is, that I would die by accident. I spent a good portion of my adult life thinking like this: that Mariko is now nine years old, almost ten, that it's seven years to adulthood and after that I can die and everything would then be okay . . . This was surely not my reaction when she was born early morning, July 21, 1978. . . . She was healthy and ours, and quickly I agreed to a new title—father. I was twenty-five, and although still full of my own childhood. . . . I was ready for parenthood."[6]

Although busy with parenthood and teaching part time, Soto was entering an extremely prolific period as a poet. His poems began to appear in prominent literary magazines such as the *New Yorker*, *Paris Review*, *Antaeus*,

Partisan Review, *Poetry*, and the *Iowa Review*. More collections of poems followed, including *The Tale of Sunlight* (1978), *Father Is a Pillow Tied to a Broom* (1980), *Where Sparrows Work Hard* (1981), *Black Hair* (1985), *Who Will Know Us?* (1990), *Home Course in Religion* (1991), *New and Selected Poems* (1995), *Junior College: Poems* (1997), *A Natural Man* (1999), *One Kind of Faith* (2003), and *A Simple Plan* (2007).

Readers as well as critics praised his works. Many critics took note of a steady growth in Soto's art and craft. Reviewer Arthur Ramirez pointed out in the summer 1981 issue of *Revista Chicano-Riquena* that "Gary Soto learned by trial and error that the creation of literary works requires craft and work, learning and progress. . . . Life, like literature, requires a great deal of work—this seems to be clear in the life and work of a leading Chicano writer."[7]

Writing in *New Letters* (September 1979), reviewer Maryfrances Wagner said of the collection *The Tale of Sunlight* that Soto "offers his reader a well-crafted collection of poetry—poems of poverty and courage revealed through the simple lives of strong characters."[8] In fact, this collection, Soto's second book, was nominated for a Pulitzer Prize, one of the highest honors given in the United States, awarded each year for outstanding achievement in journalism or literature. Gary Soto was one of the first Mexican Americans to be so honored.

Soto continued to use poetry to explore the world in which had grown up. The poems in *The Tale of Sunlight*, for example, focus on a child named Molina as well as on the owner of a Mexican bar, Manuel Zaragosa. *Black Hair* zeroes in on Soto's friends and family. In these poems, he looks back fondly at the times he shared with friends as a teenager and the time he was currently spending with his daughter. Some critics felt this collection was not as strong as his previous collections, that his first two books were major achievements, and that *Black Hair* felt distinctly minor in comparison.

Other critics disagreed. In the *Voice Literary Supplement*, Ellen Lesser praised Soto's poetic tone, "the quality of the voice, the immediate, human presence that breathes through the lines."[9] In the *Christian Science Monitor*, Tom D'Evelyn said that, with this collection, "Somehow Gary Soto has become not an important Chicano poet but an important American poet. More power to him."[10]

The critical response to the collection may have been mixed, but one poem in particular grabbed the attention of both critics and readers alike. "Oranges" is a poem of first love. With simple, direct language—"The first time I walked/With a girl, I was twelve,/Cold, and weighted

Did you know...

Soto's daughter, Mariko Heidi, graduated from Cornell University in the year 2002 with a degree in veterinary medicine. Soto's wife, Carolyn, is a hat designer!

down/With two oranges in my jacket"[11]—the poem struck a chord with its readers. Everybody has fallen in love, and everyone has been nervous about it. By once again telling his own story, Soto made it universal.

The poem "Oranges" quickly became Soto's most popular poem—and indeed, as he pointed out, one of the most popular poems by any American poet. To date, the poem has been anthologized in more than 200 different textbooks and anthologies.

In fact, one of Soto's most prestigious achievements as a poet is that he is one of the youngest poets to be included in the *Norton Anthology of Modern Poetry.* This collection of poems includes some of the best contemporary poetry published in English. Three of Soto's poems are included in the anthology.

Like any writer, Soto has also had his share of criticism. In an interview, legendary literary critic Harold Bloom told a story about a friend of his, an English professor at the University of Chicago, who wanted to replace the stories of Ernest Hemingway with the works of Gary Soto in her introductory literature course. In the interview, Bloom said, "Now Hemingway, at his very best . . . [was] about as good as a short-story writer can be. While Gary Soto couldn't write his way out of a paper bag."[12]

How does a writer respond to comments like that? As Soto said in an e-mail interview,

> Harold Bloom is a very smart reader and, in truth, I do admire his mind. . . . His response to my work, however, was unfortunate for both me and him. I do not harbor a dislike for the old master. We're both advocates of reading—he for close reading of classics and I for young people picking up books and making them part of their lives.[13]

Ironically, Soto was also on occasion criticized by his fellow Chicano writers. Some felt that he should use his poetry to more directly address the social and political issues that were part of being Mexican American. As Soto pointed out in an interview with *Ploughshares*, "There were a lot of people who couldn't quite understand what I was doing. They'd say, 'Hey, man, how come you're not talking about things that are political?' I was really groping at the time, and if I had gotten lost in that, I don't think I would have recovered."[14]

Soto realized that, by examining the individual experiences of his life and not getting involved in the temporary political fights and squabbles of the day, his poetry would have a more universal, timeless quality. The popularity of poems such as "Oranges" proved that his instincts were correct.

GIVING SOMETHING BACK

From the beginning of his career, Soto wanted to give something back and help other aspiring writers. One of his first projects was the Chicano Chapbook Series. In an interview with Momotombo Press, Soto described the project's origins:

> In Fall 1977, I met Lorna Dee Cervantes, then an unpublished poet, when I was invited by San Jose State College to do a reading. I recall traveling up from Fresno, where I was living with my wife. We had just returned home from Mexico City, more or less broke, so the $200.00 that I was paid was a godsend. After my reading (about six lonely souls showed up), we had beers, and in our dreamy state—Lorna was twenty-one, I was twenty-five—we talked literary shop. We talked about starting a magazine or publication and then went our separate ways.

> The next time I saw her was at the Reno Club in Sacramento, scene of one of the rowdiest poetry readings ever. I recall reading a story of mine called "Ronnie and Joey". . . . I remember being drunk (Two-Beers Soto, they called me), and the entire bar laughing not at what I thought was a great comic story but because my zipper was down or something. . . . It was a cool night.[15]

Soto and Cervantes knew what they wanted to do. As Soto said in the Momotombo Press interview, "Publishing outlets for Chicano writers at the time were few and far between. I figured why not publish chapbooks, a stylish sort of calling card of who you were."[16] Imagine what it must have felt like for Soto to be able to do this. When he first started out as a poet, he dreamed of the day when he could have a chapbook of his own poems published. Now, he would be able to help other Chicano writers get their start!

Twelve chapbooks were published over the next two years. Soto often had extra money in his pocket because of his teaching position, so he would personally pay the publishing costs. Many aspiring writers, including Sandra Cisneros and Alberto Rios, got their starts with Soto's chapbooks. The series has now become a collector's item—the Sandra Cisneros chapbook, *Bad Boys*, sells for more than $500—if you can even find one!

Things were going well for Soto. He had a wife and daughter he adored. He was becoming a well-respected and well-known poet. He wrote reviews and did a lengthy biographical study of Chicano poet Luis Omar Salinas. Through the Chicano Chapbook Series, he was able to help other Chicano writers get their own start. Soto, though, was not one to settle into a rut. He needed new writing challenges. Starting in 1985, he would discover a new outlet for his talents.

Soto's first published work of prose was Living Up the Street, *a book of vignettes that he termed "narrative recollection with very little commentary."*

6

From Poetry to Prose

SOTO DECIDED THAT it was time to stop writing poetry exclusively and to try his hand at prose. The two are, of course, almost completely different styles of writing. How exactly are they different?

In some ways, prose is easy to define. It is generally written in paragraphs and is usually close to the patterns of everyday speech. The word *prose*, in fact, comes from the Latin *prosa*, meaning "straightforward." Indeed, prose is, in essence, the ordinary language that people use in speaking or writing.

Poetry, on the other hand, is harder to define. The Web site Thinkquest.org defines poetry like this:

> Traditional poetry is language arranged in lines, with a regular rhythm and often a definite rhyme scheme. Nontraditional poetry does away with regular rhythm and rhyme, although it is usually set up in lines [rather than paragraphs]. The richness of its suggestions, the sounds of its words, and the strong feelings evoked by its line are often said to be what distinguish poetry from other forms of literature.

This definition sounds very specific, but the site goes on to say, "Poetry is difficult to define, but most people know when they read it."[1]

Soto himself described the differences in a phone interview:

> Poetry . . . it's like Dutch paintings. They're a small, miniscule portion of the world. They're portraits of the world, very exact, and like those, you can actually read a poem and see a wonderful picture. And through those pictures you can get a larger view.
>
> Prose . . . is not a large departure. They're all narrative, with different characters and settings involved. Prose does have much looser language. You can make a lot more mistakes in prose than you can in poetry. In poetry, if you make one or two little mistakes, people can see there's something wrong. Prose narrative is long and complex, poetry . . . not so much.[2]

Soto had several reasons to expanding his literary efforts into the world of prose. The first two reasons were practical: He was coming up for tenure in the English department at the University of California at Berkeley, and he thought that he should demonstrate his prose talent.

Another reason to start writing prose was to test himself and his abilities as a writer. He knew that he could write poetry and write it well, but prose? Soto was eager for another challenge.

The third reason to try his hand at prose was simply a desire for a new, larger audience. He knew that, no matter how good his poetry was, the audience for poetry in the United States was extremely limited. Like almost any artist, Soto was eager to have his work read by as large an audience as possible. He said in an e-mail interview, "I mean, who was reading poetry? Mine sold poorly, as does the work of most poets. But with prose? People buy and devour novels, short stories, essays, etc."[3]

Perhaps somewhat surprisingly, Soto did not find a big difference between writing prose and poetry. In an interview, he pointed out, "My poetry was often narrative, and the move from poetry to prose was effortless and warranted."[4] As he said in his interview with *Ploughshares*, "I felt [with prose], that I could be louder, more direct, also sloppier, whereas with poetry, I believed you had to control your statement, not be so obvious."[5]

Although the style of writing may have been different, the subject matter remained the same. Soto's first book of prose, *Living Up the Street*, was, like much of his poetry, personal and autobiographical. He realized that, for this direct look at his childhood, prose was the right choice, because, as he put it, "prose was needed to outline the pain and beauty of his Mexican American childhood."[6]

Indeed, as Soto pointed out in an unpublished 1988 interview, *Living Up the Street* was intended to be

> a set of narrative recollections with very little commentary. I would rather show and not tell about certain levels of poverty, of childhood; I made a conscious effort not to tell anything

> but just present the stories and let the reader come up with assumptions about the book—just show not tell, which is what my poetry has been doing for years and years.[7]

The book was written in longhand at his dining table and is subtitled "Narrative Recollections." Indeed, each chapter is a short vignette, a memory drawn from his childhood. The chapter entitled "Fear," for example, examines Soto's memories of a school bully. The piece "1, 2, 3" looks back at one summer spent at the neighborhood playground. Another story, "Black Hair," reveals the anger that Soto felt when he realized that, because his younger stepbrother was brown skinned, he would never be considered attractive by the standards of the time.

The book could not be published by his usual publisher, which specialized in poetry. How was Soto, still unknown outside poetry circles, going to get it published? His wife provided the answer. She was taking a class with the idea of going into publishing herself. It turned out that the teacher of the class had a small publishing company of his own and jumped at the chance to publish Soto's book. Although the company was a small commercial publishing house, the book quickly came to the attention of readers and became an underground classic, sold by word of mouth as friends told other friends about the book. *Living Up the Street* has since been purchased by a much larger publishing house and has become Soto's largest-selling title, now in its thirty-fifth printing.

Critics as well as readers loved the book. In the *San Francisco Review of Books*, Geoffrey Dunn stated that:

> Soto has changed literary forms, though he returns once again to the dusty fields and industrial alleyways of his Fresno childhood . . . *Living Up the Street* is certainly a formidable

> work by one of America's more gifted and sensitive writers. The 21 autobiographical short stories (or, more accurately, vignettes) assembled here recall with amazing detail the day-to-day traumas, tragedies, and occasional triumphs of growing up brown in the American Southwest.[8]

With reviews like that, it's no wonder that *Living Up the Street* earned Soto the prestigious American Book Award. That same year, Sandra Cisneros, whose chapbook Soto had published, received an American Book Award as well, for her book *The House on Mango Street*.

The success of *Living Up the Street* led to additional works of autobiographical prose. *Small Faces* was published in 1986, followed by *Lesser Evils: Ten Quartets* in 1988, and *A Summer Life* in 1990. In 2001, many of the essays originally published in *Small Faces* and *Lesser Evils*, as well as some new material, were compiled in a single volume, *The Effects of Knut Hamsun on a Fresno Boy*.

The books were all critically well received. Writing in the *Bloomsbury Review*, Alicia Fields pointed out that

Did you know...

Knut Hamsun (1859–1952), was a leading Norwegian author and winner of the Nobel Prize for Literature in 1920. His work and his life as a starving writer had a major influence on Soto. In the title essay in his collection *The Effects of Knut Hamsun on a Fresno Boy*, Soto discussed reading Knut Hamsun's novel *Hunger* and beginning to see himself as a writer of prose as well as poetry.

Knut Hamsun, a Norwegian writer, won the Nobel Prize for Literature in 1920. When Soto read Hamsun's novel Hunger, *he identified with Hamsun's own experiences as a boy growing up in poverty and later as an artist struggling to get by.*

"although *Small Faces* contains stories about major events in the author's life . . . this is primarily a book about small but telling moments."[9] A reviewer for *Booklist* said of *Lesser Evils: Ten Quartets* that "the collection shows a writer who is becoming more reflective as he matures, making sober observations about women, marriage, pets, parenthood, teaching, writing, responsibility."[10]

A Summer Life, the fourth of Soto's collections of reminiscences, offers 39 short essays that "make up a compelling biography" of Soto's youth, according to Ernesto Trejo in the *Los Angeles Times Book Review*. Trejo goes on to say that, in *A Summer Life*, as in his previous collections, Soto "holds the past up to memory's probing flashlight, turns it around ever so carefully, and find in the smallest of incidents the occasion for literature."[11]

Indeed, in all of his autobiographical works, Soto uses small incidents of everyday life to bring the reader into his world. As pointed out in a biography posted on the Web site www.notablebiographies.com, "Readers are introduced to Soto's neighborhood through snapshot descriptions of family, friends, sights, sounds and smells."[12] Soto's memory of his past, his ability to describe in detail the color of a hated jacket or the way his grandmother looked sipping coffee and eating a Danish, is part of what makes his writing so unmistakably his own.

This ability to remember the past and what it was like to be a child, along with a growing appreciation for the joy as well as the pain of barrio life, would serve him well in the next stage of his career. Little did Soto know that he was soon to begin reaching readers in numbers he had never thought possible. He was about to enter the world of writing for children.

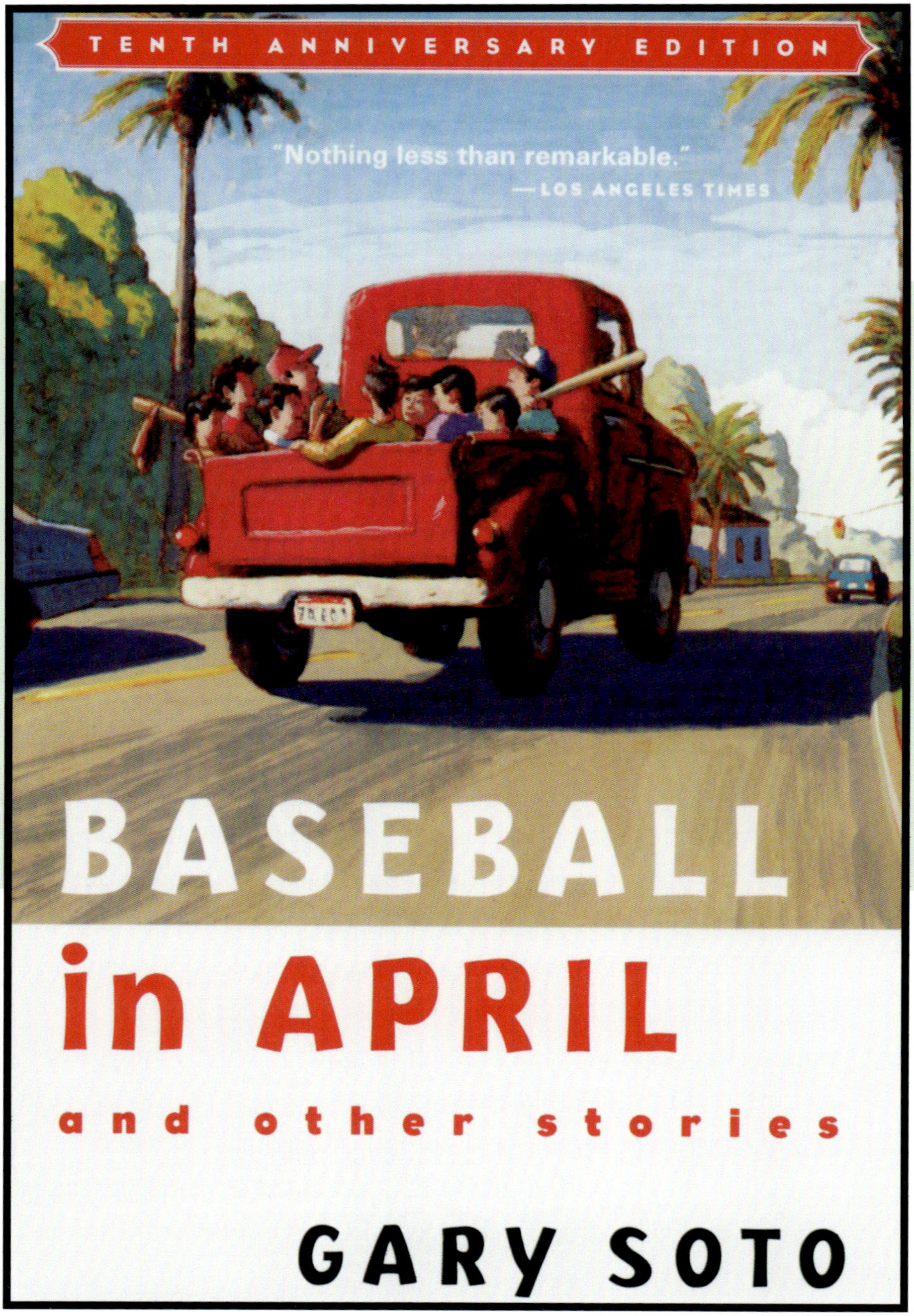

Gary Soto's first book of stories for children, Baseball in April, *was published in 1990. The collection contains 11 stories, each featuring a different character, which have in common their similar settings: poor neighborhoods in central California.*

7

Writing for Kids

TO SOTO, WRITING for children seemed to be the next logical step in his career. After the publication of *Living Up the Street*, he began to meet his readers, many of whom were Mexican American. These fans told him how much his work meant to them as Mexican Americans. They identified with his story and through his story were able to see their own stories in print for the first time.

Along with the fans came fan letters from teenage readers across the country. They told Soto how much they appreciated his work and suggested to him that he would make a great children's book author. With his understanding of childhood and of what it is like growing up in poorer neighborhoods, they thought he would be a natural.

Always eager to take up a new writing challenge, Soto agreed. He knew that the subjects that he wrote about for an adult audience—family, childhood, growing up, and coming of age in Fresno—could be tailored for a younger audience as well.

One other aspect of writing for children excited him. When Soto was growing up, virtually no available children's literature described the Mexican-American experience. He hoped to change that. In his books for children and young adults, he wanted to explore the lives of young Chicanos. As he said in his *Booklist* biography, he hoped that by doing so he could "start Chicanos reading."[1]

Soto hoped that his books for children and young adults would differ from those previously written. Although he appreciated and enjoyed many of those, he wanted his books to reflect what he had learned about writing through his poetry. He addressed the topic in an essay, "On the Particulars of the World":

> I am new to children's writing and am only now getting to know some of the books in the field. What has struck me, now that I am reading YA adults, is that despite their other literary merits, the writing has so little that is obviously regional, obviously bent on nailing down a life that is wholly particular. Seldom are real rivers mentioned, or mountains, gangs, streets, cars; in short, the particulars of the world. Seldom do place names matter, names ringing of the familiar, such as Avocado Lake, Pinedale, Academy Cemetery, Francher's Creek, real names that might give rise to a reader's dreaming state of mind and curiosity for a faraway place. For the most part the novels I have been reading are homogeneous and wide-spread in their feelings

> and cast of characters. They lack a sense of place. The stories could happen anywhere. And they often happen in a way that doesn't exclude anyone by race, this, in a way, satisfying the book market, but also, in a way, dissatisfying any reader who knows what the real world is like. The characters are interchangeable, racially, that is.
>
> I suppose because I was first trained as a poet and was told repeatedly to go to the particular—your block, your family, your friends, some dirt pile in the backyard—that I wrote about my hometown, Fresno, California. And then, more particularly, I looked to the southeast area of Fresno—the Roosevelt High area—the industrial area of south Fresno where I grew up. My characters are Mexican-American, mostly play-ground kids, mostly the people of children whose parents work for Color Tile or a Safeway distribution center. I'm beginning to think that children's writing could learn to see regionality and particularity as under-explored territory. I'm beginning to think we don't have to satisfy everyone. We can remember the adult writers . . . who had tenderness and longing toward place, even if that place scared the hell out of them when they were young.[2]

Like his poetry, Soto's books for younger readers, whether picture books or novels for young adults, are fully grounded in the specific. One of Soto's greatest talents as a writer is his ability to paint pictures with words. This allows the reader to see very clearly what he is describing. The settings, the details, all the little things that Soto sees and depicts in his books, like in his poetry, help the reader fully experience whatever the character is experiencing.

Everything that Soto had learned as a writer went into his children's books. He said in an e-mail interview, "I had been preparing myself for writing fiction, as for seven years I had been writing personal essays that were narrative in nature. And, again, a lot of my poems were narrative."[3] No matter what Soto is writing, though, one can always detect the poet. Soto himself acknowledged this in discussing his books of essays: "Anyone reading these . . . will see the poet within the prose."[4]

Once the decision was made to start writing for children, the books quickly began to appear in bookstores and libraries. His first collection of stories for children, the award-winning *Baseball in April and Other Stories,* appeared in 1990.

SUCCESSFUL CHILDREN'S AUTHOR

Baseball in April contains 11 stories, each featuring a different character. They are linked by setting: poorer neighborhoods in central California. One of the first stories Soto wrote was the title story. In it, two brothers play baseball for a neighborhood team when they both fail to make the Little League team for the third year in a row. (This story, entitled "Baseball in April," saw its genesis in one of Soto's earliest poems and then later appeared as an essay with the same name in the collection *Living Up the Street*, before finally becoming a short story.)

Other stories entered more unfamiliar territory. In the story "Mother and Daughter," the main character, Yollie, needs money to buy a new dress for the eighth-grade dance. This was the first time Soto had written from the viewpoint of a female character, but a reader would never know it. Whether Soto is writing about men or women, young or old, his love and compassion for his characters shines through.

His favorite story in the collection is entitled "Two Dreamers." In it, nine-year-old Hector's grandfather, Luis Molina, dreams of becoming rich by buying a house, fixing it up, and reselling it. Unable to speak much English, Luis relies on his grandson to make phone calls and communicate for him with the outside, English-speaking world. "I think it captured a Mexican family very well," Soto said in a phone interview. "The dreams about getting rich in America. The kid not understanding the grandfather's need to understand the price of the house. There was just something there that I liked."[5]

There was something in *Baseball in April and Other Stories* that a lot of people liked. The book sold extremely well, and the critics raved about Soto's first attempt at children's fiction. The *Los Angeles Times Book Review* said that "Soto's sensitivity to young people's concerns and his ability to portray the world as it is perceived by children is nothing less than remarkable."[6] *The Boston Globe* raved that it was "a fine collection of stories that offers a different cultural perspective about feelings common to all teenagers. Soto writes well and with tremendous insight into the process of growing up."[7]

Perhaps most important to Soto, many reviewers noted that, although the stories were about Mexican Americans, the themes were universal. The *Horn Book* said,

> Gary Soto is an astute observer of the desires, fears, and foibles of children and teenagers going about the business of daily living. In these eleven vignettes featuring Mexican-American families, the character portrayals are gentle; the tone is quiet and somewhat bittersweet; and respect for family is a consistent value. This illumination of the everyday will strike chords of recognition in readers of all ages.[8]

Roger Sutton wrote in the *Bulletin of the Center for Children's Books* that the "stories are told with tenderness, optimism and wry humor." He went on to add that Chicano readers "will be pleased to find a book that admits larger possibilities than the stereotypes of the noble-but-destitute farm worker," but that kids from all cultures also "will feel like part of this neighborhood."[9]

Baseball in April also received its share of awards. It was named a *Booklist* Editor's Choice and a *Horn Book* Fanfare Selection. The American Library Association named it a Best Book for Young Adults. Given the awards and the enthusiastic response of critics and readers, Soto knew that writing for children was a perfect match for his talents.

Soto had always been a prolific writer, but after he started to write children's books, his output greatly increased. By the mid 1990s, he was writing as many as three children's books a year, in addition to his work for adults. He also wrote books for children of all ages and reading levels. He wrote books of poetry, including *A Fire in My Hands* (1991), *Neighborhood Odes* (1992), *Canto Familiar* (1997), *Fearless Fernie* (2002), and *Worlds Apart* (2005).

He also wrote picture books for very young children, such as *Too Many Tamales* (1992), *If the Shoe Fits* (2002), and the Chato the cat tales: *Chato's Kitchen* (1995), *Chato and the Party Animals* (2000), and *Chato Goes Cruisin'* (2005). Along with those are chapter books for kids in middle school, including the titles *The Skirt* (1992), *The Pool Party* (1993), and *Boys at Play* (1995); young adult novels such as *Taking Sides* (1991), *Crazy Weekend* (1994), *Buried Onions* (1997), and *The Afterlife* (2003); adult poetry and novels; two plays for children; two biographies; and even one opera.

As one can imagine, Soto was rapidly devoting more and more of his time to writing. He finally reached the decision

Chato the cat is Soto's favorite character. He appears in three books: Chato's Kitchen, Chato and the Party Animals, *and* Chato Goes Cruisin'. *Soto is proud of Chato because he is sympathetic and playful, but also has a slight "hard edge."*

that it was necessary to quit teaching and focus on being a full-time writer. His daughter, Mariko, was 16 and nearly grown. Soto had, as he had hoped, "got the job done" in raising her. Fortunately for Soto, unlike most other writers, he was in a position to financially support himself by his writing alone. Now, he could do what he wanted to do most.

There were other reasons behind his decision to leave his position at the University of California, Berkeley. He had become tired of fighting the university to hire more Chicanos and of the politics and conflicts among faculty and the administration. As he described it in his essay "Getting It Done," in the collection *The Effects of Knut Hamsun on a Fresno Boy*:

> The end of my teaching career began suddenly when, during a faculty meeting, the faces of my colleagues underwent a frightening metamorphosis. They began to resemble various chicken parts—breast, thighs, wings—muffled behind the sheen of Saran Wrap . . . that was the beginning of the end for me, and two years later, after other surrealistic hot flashes and dark cloudlike drifts of depression, I quit teaching altogether. After my last class, I literally jogged off the Cal Berkeley campus, arms hugging bundles of teaching evaluations after thirteen years of rubbing my bottom on hard chairs. Happy that my books were selling, I took the beautiful redneck stance of "Take this job and shove it!"[10]

COMMON THEMES

Although Soto writes for all age groups, from beginning readers to adults, his subject matter and themes remain constant. He writes about families, both fictional and real. He writes about growing up, both in his own experience and that of his fictional characters. He writes about the damage that growing up poor can do, both to himself and his family and to his characters. Of course, he also writes about the joys as well as the sorrows of growing up Mexican American in the United States.

One additional feature links the majority of Soto's work—a glossary at the back of the book. In many of his books, Soto sprinkles the speech of his characters with the Spanish words that they would be likely to use, no matter how fluent they are in English. Most English speakers will be able to figure out what the words mean in English because of how they are used in the sentence, but Soto includes a glossary of translations at the end of each book just in case.

Another of Soto's gifts is his ability to match his style to his audience. He never talks down to his audience, no matter what their age. His respect for his reader and his love for his characters are evident in every sentence, and no matter what reading level he is writing for, from beginning readers to adults, every sentence is undeniably Gary Soto. His way of seeing and his poetic voice emerge clearly in his prose.

Writing novels for young adults gives Soto the time and space necessary to examine some of these topics and themes in greater detail than in his stories and poetry. The novel *Taking Sides* (1991), for example, tells the story of eighth-grader Lincoln Mendoza. He has recently moved with his mother from an inner-city neighborhood (similar to that in which Soto grew up) to a predominantly Anglo, or white, suburb of Fresno. The length of a novel gave Soto the time necessary to examine Lincoln's torn loyalties more fully: the friends and life he had to give up and his new life and friends. A writer for *Kirkus Reviews* felt that, in *Taking Sides*, Soto "creates a believable, compelling picture of the stress that racial prejudice places on minority children."[11]

In a *School Library Journal* review, Bruce Anne Shook described it as a "light but appealing story" that "deals with cultural differences, moving, and basketball."[12]

The book was so popular that the character of Lincoln Mendoza made a second appearance in the novel *Pacific Crossing*. In it, Lincoln and his best friend from his old neighborhood, Tony, face cultural challenges when they go to Japan as exchange students. Once there, Lincoln learns that, external differences aside, life in Japan is not that different from that at home. *Horn Book*'s Ellen Fader said that the novel "highlighted the truisms that people are the same all over the world and that friends can be found anywhere, if one makes the effort."[13]

One of Soto's most popular and critically acclaimed novels for young adults is *Buried Onions* (1997). The book is about 19-year-old Eddie, who is trying to escape the poverty and crime of life in the barrio by taking vocational classes. When his cousin is murdered, his aunt tries to convince Eddie to kill his cousin's murderer. This is something that Eddie just cannot do—he knows that if he takes that step into violence, his life will be over and he will never be able to escape to something better. At the end of the book, with a gang member looking for him and all of his money gone, Eddie joins the military in the hope that he can find a better life.

Critics praised the book's realistically bleak view of barrio life. In *Kirkus Reviews*, a critic said that "in bleak sentences of whispered beauty, Eddie tells how he dropped out of vocational college and is attempting to get by with odd jobs." The critic goes on to say that this "unrelenting portrait is unsparing in squalid details . . . [and] one that makes no concessions."[14]

Soto himself was pleased with the book. As he said in an e-mail interview:

> I wrote *Jesse* (1994), I liked it, and I didn't get good reviews. I thought I was going to win an award for it, but nothing. So I though I'd do something less sweet, and I thought about gangs, and thought I'd do something called *Buried Onions*, working with the metaphor that buried underneath Fresno there's a layer of onions that causes everyone to weep and cry. What was sweet in *Jesse* became stronger in *Buried Onions*. The protagonist who's a little ornery, not as sweet and naïve as Jesse is.[15]

Six years later, Soto returned to the world of *Buried Onions* for the novel *The Afterlife*. In the book's first pages, the character of Jesus, known as Chuy, is at a school dance. While in the bathroom combing his hair, he tells the guy standing next to him that he likes his yellow shoes. Unfortunately for Chuy, the guy in the yellow shoes takes his comment the wrong way and stabs him to death. It takes several pages before the reader realizes that Chuy is the cousin who was killed in *Buried Onions*.

The Afterlife is told from the perspective of Chuy's ghost, which roams the streets of Fresno visiting the friends and family who mourn him, including his mother, who seeks to avenge his death. As the book progresses, Chuy's ghostly body slowly begins to disappear and he comes to realize that, although his life was short, it was worth living.

It is interesting that it was seven years before Soto sat down to write the sequel to *Buried Onions*. He explained the process in an interview posted on his publisher's Web site, www.harcourtbooks.com:

> I think writers pick up on details that may haunt them. They turn these over and over because they never seem satisfied and can't get enough of them. The same here in this novel. I could have been satisfied with *Buried Onions*, the prequel

> to *The Afterlife,* and believed that that story was done. But, I wanted to go back to the earlier novel and re-experience the tragedy of a young man's death, the kind of death, I believe, that happens daily throughout our country. Young men—and women—are dying for insignificant reasons, a remark or gesture which gives offense to another. Of course, in *The Afterlife* I view "yellow shoes" as cowardice and "onions" as a vapor that makes someone weep.[16]

There was another reason for Soto to write *The Afterlife* as well—the subject of ghosts in his own life. As Soto continued in his Web site interview:

> My father died when I was five, and there were reports that he came back as a spirit. I recall my Uncle Shorty telling of when he used to bathe after work, he would hear gravel crunch in our backyard and become so startled that his body would freeze from fear. It was my father returning from that first journey called death. My brother has had the same experience as well. In his case, our uncle Frank appeared at the foot of his bed and was smiling and giggling and saying everything was okay where he then dwelled. But where [did] Chuy go? Into the memories of those family and friends, the survivors. . . . I think our actions linger after we are gone.[17]

Oddly enough, considering that the book is about death, *The Afterlife* is, ultimately, hopeful. As *Publisher's Weekly* pointed out in its review:

> Soto concocts an ingenious way of introducing tension to the story: Chuy's astral body is disappearing bit by bit, and as the tale ends, so does the audience's knowledge of Chuy's ultimate destiny. The premise could sound dark and morose, but the novel is instead filled with hope and elegance. The

> author counterbalances difficult ideas with moments of genuine tenderness as well as a provocative lesson about the importance of savoring every moment—a lesson that Chuy, once fretful and insecure, comes to understand.[18]

Although to date, Soto has written more than 30 books for children and young adults, it is one of his earlier, lesser-known works, *Jesse* (1994), which remains his personal favorite, despite its lack of popular success. (This lack of success led to Soto's writing *Buried Onions*.)

Jesse is perhaps Soto's most revealing and autobiographical work. Eager to escape his alcoholic stepfather, Jesse, 17 years old, leaves high school and moves in with his older brother, Abel, to take classes at Fresno City College. The year is 1968, and politics are always in the air as Jesse and Abel are forced to contend with the possibility of being drafted to fight in Vietnam, as well as becoming involved with César Chávez and his United Farm Workers movement. Poverty is an ongoing presence: The boys work as day laborers in the fields, picking melons, oranges, or cotton—whatever they can do to pay the rent and keep food on the table.

As Joel Shoemaker said in the *School Library Journal*:

> The story is poignant, pregnant with unfulfilled promise and dreams of a future that is hoped for but rarely imagined. Simple words reveal universal experiences; innocent and open, Jesse begins to see the real world and discover his place in it. The ending is a bit bleak, suggesting the likelihood of more of the same mindless, backbreaking, spirit-crushing work, with a plethora of unknowns lurking just over the horizon. Readers looking for a finely written, contemplative narrative will appreciate this work.[19]

Other critics agreed. In *Booklist*, Merri Monks said:

> Jesse is artistically gifted and shy around girls; his struggles to communicate with girls, to date, and to succeed both academically in school transcend the specifics of race and class. But Soto's story of a particular Mexican American boy in Fresno, California, during the height of the Vietnam War is rich in the details of Jesse's life and culture—his friendships with other Mexican Americans, his involvement in Cesar Chavez's farm workers' movement, his struggles to find himself and a meaningful life in spite of the limits placed on him by poverty and prejudice. All in all, a highly readable novel.[20]

In *Jesse*, Gary Soto took aspects of his own life and transformed them into art. In this book, he achieved his goal as a writer—to take the specific and make it universal. Despite the book's lack of popular success (or perhaps *because* of it), as Soto said in an interview, "I think it's still my favorite. It's not that it's autobiographical. There's a tone there that is very sweet, something naïve, I think the tone of the novel is special. . . . I remember writing it, knowing, getting a sense that *this* was the real thing. I knew that this was going to be an important book for me, personally."[21]

This is not to say that all of Soto's young adult novels are serious, thought-provoking books. *Crazy Weekend* (1994), for example, is a fast-paced comedic thriller about two teenagers from East Los Angeles. Hector and his best friend, Mando, travel to Fresno to spend the weekend with Hector's uncle, Julio. While assisting Julio in his photography work, the boys witness an armed robbery in progress. When the robbers find out that the boys are witnesses, they decided to pursue Hector and Mando. Critics and readers enjoyed the book's mixture of laughs and thrills. *Publisher's Weekly* called it "a winning combination of a thriller and a comedy . . . an entertaining novel, especially for contemporaries of these hip, likable protagonists."[22] The book was so popular that a sequel, *Summer on Wheels,* was published in 1995. In it, the two heroes take an eight-day bike trip from East Los Angeles to Santa Monica. Needless to say, the boys are kept on their toes by a series of comical adventures and misadventures.

OTHER GENRES

Since the publication of *Baseball in April and Other Stories*, two more collections of short stories have followed: *Local News* (1993) and *Petty Crimes* (1998). Both collections showcase Soto's growing confidence as a writer of fiction and his continued willingness to take chances in his stories.

Local News contains 11 tales of growing up Chicano in California. Each of the stories looks at situations common to most people growing up. "First Job" looks at what can go wrong on Alex's first job of raking leaves. "El Radio" is the story of two teenage girls who have a small party when Patricia's parents are away from home. "Nickel-a-Pound Plane Ride" is the story of Araceli and what happens when achieving your dream turns out to be a disappointment.

School Library Journal praised Soto's ability to

> use his ability to see the story in everyday experiences, and to create ordinary, distinctly individual and credible characters to charm readers into another world. . . . The book will be as popular as a collection of stories about young people as it will be useful for starting discussions regarding sibling rivalry, self-image, cultures, or writing styles."[23]

Petty Crimes goes even further and deeper in its examination of the lives of young Mexican Americans. The stories include topics such as dealing with bullies, petty thievery, dealing with grandparents who have Alzheimer's, and even a girl trying to buy back her dead mother's clothes.

The opening story, "La Güera," shows Soto's bravery as a writer in featuring a protagonist who is not particularly likable. The opening scenes show Priscilla as a little girl in kindergarten; by sixth grade she is calling herself "La Güera" (a name that means something like "paleface" or "whitey"), teasing her hair, wearing too much makeup, and constantly stealing. Her mother sends her to her aunt and cousins in the country for a summer visit, but she finds herself unable or unwilling to change. At the end of the story, La Güera is back in the city, getting into a vicious fight with another girl. The story does not offer much hope for La Güera's future, but it does help the reader understand why she is what she is and to at least feel compassion for her.

As Soto said in a phone interview, "I know they're [the protagonists] not nice. My earlier collections tended to be really sweet, so I wanted to write one that was a little more worldly. I think it's one of my strongest collections of stories."[24] *Petty Crimes* won Soto the prestigious PEN Center West Book Award.

One of Soto's favorite stories is included in the collection *Help Wanted* (2005). The story, "Teenage Chimps," is another bold step forward for Soto. Soto has long realized that teenagers often feel out of place, ugly, and awkward—as if they do not fit in anywhere. In the story, the protagonists literally see themselves as chimps. As the character Ronnie described it, "One morning I woke up craving bananas. When I jumped out of bed, I noticed that my arms hung a little closer to the ground. *Dang* I thought, as I walked, arms dragging, to the bathroom. . . . I had known ever since I was a little kid that I wasn't going to grow up to be a *GQ* model but a monkey."[25]

Soto takes pride in all of his work, but he feels a particular pride in this story. "That's a serious story. I look at all my work, and I think that's a real story. It's about loneliness; it's about self doubt in boys . . . that can be scary, you know? They're teenage chimps. In fact, I liked it so much that there's a sequel coming out, a novel. It turned out good. One chimp boy falls in love with a girl."[26]

"Teenage Chimps" may be his favorite story, but Soto's favorite character has appeared in three of his picture books for young readers. He is a feline named Chato, and he is literally the coolest cat in East Los Angeles. Soto enjoys him because "he has a little . . . hard edge to him. Not a real hard edge, he's still sympathetic, very playful. I'm happy with the character."[27]

Chato made his first appearance in *Chato's Kitchen* (1995), along with his best buddy, Novio Boy. They try to lure the *ratoncitos*—little mice living across the street—over for dinner of fajitas, frijoles, and enchiladas. Little do the mice realize that the cats plan to have the mice

Did you know...

Gary Soto's favorite poem is "My Cat Jeoffry" by Christopher Smart (1722–1771). This poem, written between 1756 and 1763 as part of a larger poem, "Jubilate Agno," consists of 74 lines in praise of the author's cat and was written while the author was in an insane asylum!

themselves for dinner! It turns out that the mice have a surprise in store for Chato and Novio Boy as well, and they all become good friends.

In *Chato and the Party Animals* (2000), Chato learns that his best friend, Novio Boy, has never had a birthday party. Chato decides to throw him the best birthday party ever. Chato arranges for cake, music, guests, and a piñata but forgets to invite Novio Boy to his own party!

Critics loved both the stories and the exuberant, colorful illustrations by Susan Guevara. In the *School Library Journal*, Ann Welton said that the book's

> rollicking language—a completely integrated and poetic combination of barrio slang, Spanish, and colloquial English—carries the story along. Guevara's lively acrylic-on-scratchboard illustrations have a verve and style that will make readers long to join the fun. A glossary of Spanish words preceding the text nearly removes any mystery, rendering this joyous celebration of friendship not only understandable but irresistible.[28]

Soto enjoys writing novels, short stories, and picture books, but at heart he is still a poet. In his four poetry collections for children, he was able to indulge his love of poetry while addressing it to younger audiences. By writing poetry about the everyday, he hopes to remove the fear that many readers have of reading poetry and turn them instead into poetry lovers. As Renee Steinberg said in the *School Library Journal*, "The rewards of well-chosen words that create vivid, sensitive images await readers of this collection of poems. Through Soto's keen eyes, they see, and will be convinced, that there is poetry in everything."[29]

"There is poetry in everything," are words to make any poet proud. That is the goal of every poet—that through his or her poetry, the reader will see the world a bit differently and will see the magic, the poetry, in everyday life. In poems such as "Tortillas Like Africa," included in the collection *Canto Familiar*, Soto does just that. The poem describes the simple preparation of tortillas: "When Isaac and me squeezed dough over a mixing bowl/When we dusted the cutting board with flour,/When we spanked our balls of dough,/When we said, 'Here goes,'/And began rolling out tortillas,/We giggled because ours came out not round,/like Mamma's,/But in the shapes of faraway lands."[30]

Soto described the poem as one of his favorites: "It's a nice, surprising poem, delicate, sort of a cultural expression; like tortillas, it's kind of a worldly food."[31] It takes a writer with Soto's talent and artistry to make the reader see a tortilla in a whole new kind of light—to realize that one can make poetry out of virtually anything.

As a writer, Soto had mastered the art of poetry, the personal essay, the novel, the short story, and even the picture book. There were still more creative challenges ahead of him, however, and with greater success came even more opportunity to give back to the community.

In 2000, Soto's biography Jessie de la Cruz: A Profile of a United Farm Worker *was published. De la Cruz was the first female United Farm Worker organizer, and Soto learned a lot about her in the many interviews he conducted in order to write his book. Above, Soto poses with de la Cruz in 2003.*

8

Politics, Plays, and Movies

UNLIKE MANY AUTHORS who have achieved success in one genre of writing and always write in that style, Gary Soto is not afraid to try other styles. Always looking for new challenges, Soto has branched off into the worlds of theater, movies, and even opera. As Soto said in an interview, "I've been successful. . . . I want to do it all!"[1]

To date, Soto has written two plays: *Novio Boy: a Play* (1997) and *Nerdlandia* (1999). The first play tells the story of Rudy, a shy ninth grader who works up the courage to ask Patricia, an eleventh grader, out on a date. She accepts, and the rest of the play shows Rudy's hilarious attempts to do everything he can to make the date a success. The second play, *Nerdlandia*, is about a character named Martin. Martin is a Mexican-American nerd who, in order to win the heart of the girl he loves, attempts to change himself into a "cool" guy. Critics and audiences enjoyed the play, and, much to Soto's surprise, the Los Angeles Opera commissioned him to write the libretto, the complete text or words, for an opera based on the play.

Soto himself has been pleased, surprised, and proud of the success of his plays. He said in an interview:

> *Nerdlandia* originally started out as a skit called "96 Tears." It was a collection of oldie but goodie songs. I wanted to do something like [the musical] *5 Guys Named Moe*, but then I found about copyright and I thought, let me just write this as a straight comedy. I did *Novio Boy* first, then I did *Nerdlandia*. I think *Nerdlandia* is the better play and I like it, but *Novio Boy* has been unbelievable. This thing has been . . . no play sells as well as *Novio Boy*! It's in its twenty-fifth printing![2]

Always ready to try something new, Soto has even tried his hand at making movies: He described in an interview how this came about:

> I was very jazzed up on getting involved with kids, and I thought, "let's make a film!" I didn't know anything about cameras, I just wrote the stories. So I brought in a camera. . . . They're very hard to make . . . VERY hard to make. I never considered myself a filmmaker. I don't think I'd want to do it again. People are mystified by film, you know, and less so by writing. Writing is a harder art. Writing is really hard.[3]

Soto claims that he did not know much about making movies, but his were still critically successful. In fact, his second film, *The Pool Party*, won the Andrew Carnegie Medal.

GIVING BACK

In an interview for *Contemporary Literary Criticism*, Soto said, "I write because there is pain in my life, our family, and those living in the San Joaquin Valley. . . . I write because those I live and work with can't write."[4] This need to give voice to the voiceless, to tell the stories that they can't tell themselves, this desire to help, drives him to help the community in other ways as well.

Since 2001, Gary Soto has been the Young People Ambassador for the United Farm Workers of America (UFWA). In this role, during his visits to libraries and schools, he introduces children to the importance of the Farm Workers movement. Soto is also the Young People Ambassador for California Rural Legal Assistance (CRLA). CRLA does vital work, extending financial and legal assistance to California's rural poor. Soto has gone on many marches and protests for these organizations, as well as for the National Farm Workers Ministry (NFWM). He does whatever he can to lend his voice in support of poor people everywhere.

Soto has not only marched with them, he has written books in support of the United Farm Workers. In 2000, his biography *Jessie de la Cruz: A Profile of a United Farm Worker* was published. It tells the story of Jessie de la Cruz, the first female organizer of the United Farm Workers. A farm worker and child of farm workers herself, de la Cruz knew firsthand the difficult working conditions that her people faced. Because of this, she worked tirelessly to encourage others to stand up for their rights, to strike when necessary to win those rights, and to work with other workers to gain

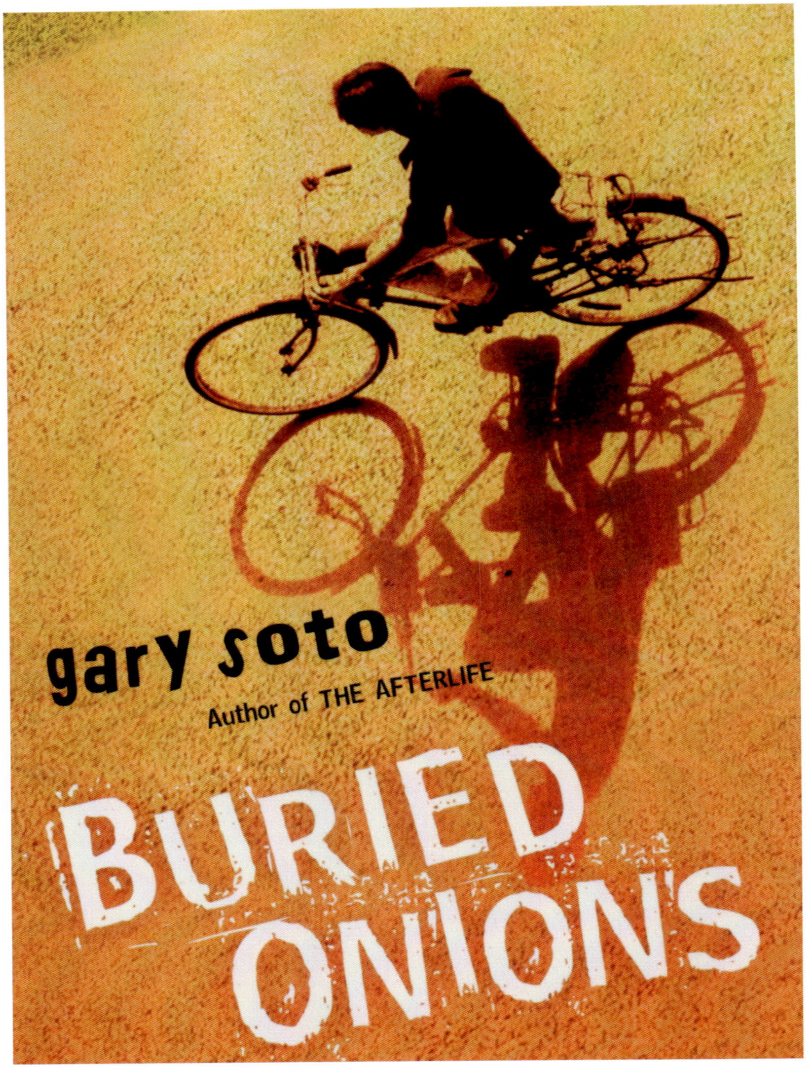

Soto's book* Buried Onions *was published in 1998. It tells the story of 19-year-old Eddie, who lives in the barrio but is desperate to make a better life for himself. When his cousin is murdered, his cousin's death haunts Eddie for the rest of his life.

better pay and working conditions for all workers. For many, Jessie de la Cruz is a true American hero.

Writing the book was a new kind of challenge for Soto. Unlike his fiction or even his personal essays, he was telling the story of a real, living person. To get it right, he spent a lot of time doing interviews and research. Also, as he said in an interview, "It was a dilemma writing a biography and keeping it interesting to younger readers. You know that biographies by nature are factual, maybe a bit about personality, and I wanted to keep it engaging to younger readers."[5]

Critics and readers alike loved the book. Perhaps most important to Soto, so did the book's subject: "Jessie liked the book. We sat down together with her sister and we went over it, to make sure things were right. Her memory is very good, it was much better a few years ago, when I wrote the book, but then, she was still very sharp. She remembered everything."[6]

Three years later, Soto wrote *Cesar Chavez: A Hero for Everyone*, aimed at third to fifth graders. In it, he was able to educate a new generation of Americans about the man he considers a personal hero:

> Cesar Chavez . . . was the most courageous person imaginable. It's difficult to explain how he charged up people during the 1960s and early 1970s. I'm from that period and recognized that his plan was a plan that would affect not only farm workers but a wide range of others. He was inspiring and today the UFW remains inspiring for a new generation.[7]

Soto serves as a role model for a generation of Chicano youth. He is deeply involved with the Coalingua-Huron-Avenal (CHA) House, Arte America, and other organizations, generously giving both his time and money to provide assistance and encouragement to Chicano students and artists. Remembering his own struggles as a young Chicano poet, Soto goes out of his way to encourage a new generation of writers, serving as a judge for numerous literary contests. In the past, he has even offered scholarships to deserving rural youths.

Giving money and judging contests is great, but Soto goes the extra mile in encouraging readers Chicano and Anglo alike. As he said in his essay "Who Is Your Reader?":

> Over a nine-year period I have spoken to three hundred thousand teachers and students, possibly more. . . . Unlike most other contemporary poets and writers, I've taken the show on the road and built a name among la gente, the people. I have ventured into schools where I have played basketball and baseball with young people, sung songs, acted in skits, delivered commencement speeches, learned three chords on a Mexican guitar to serenade teachers. . . . I have gone to prisons and mingled with people who have done time. . . . My readership is strung from large cities, such as Los Angeles, to dinky Del Rey where peach trees outnumber the population by many thousands. . . . My business is to make readers from non-readers."[8]

Did you know...

César Chávez (1927–1993), was a farm worker, labor leader, and activist who dedicated his life to improving the lives of those who work on America's farms. Along with Dolores Huerta, he founded the National Farm Workers Association, which evolved into the United Farm Workers of today. The union, led by Chávez, organized strikes and boycotts to bring about higher wages and better working conditions for farm workers. Today, Chávez's birthday is a holiday in several states in America, and many parks, libraries, schools, and streets are named in his honor.

BEING A WRITER

Obviously, Soto has a busy life. Still, most important to him, the center of who he is, is being a writer. His life revolves around that; it is the main part of his daily routine. As Soto said, "I wake up, drink two cups of coffee, and get writing. I work from 8:30 until about 2:00 P.M., then do some exercises such as [playing] bad tennis."[9] Soto has even earned his black belt in tae kwon do.

In fact, he has been a long time practitioner of martial arts, since his days of wrestling in high school. One might wonder what would attract a poet to such sports, but as Soto explained in an interview:

> Karate offered power, pure and simple. That is why so many *first* gravitate towards martial arts; however in a serious system you learn a deeper meaning of the art. You also discover friendships among the practitioners. Wrestling was just a way to get involved with school life. It was the only sport I *could* make. [I was] too small for football and too short for basketball. Baseball? No hitting or fielding.[10]

Gary Soto has obviously come a long way from his days of picking grapes in the fields outside of Fresno. He has become one the country's leading writers and an inspiration to young Chicano writers everywhere. He was able to do this only because he was fortunate enough to discover his passion, to find his gift. As he said in an unpublished interview in 1988, "This [writing] is my one talent. There are a lot of people who never discover what their talent is. . . . I am very lucky to have found mine."[11]

Because Soto is able to speak directly to the aspirations and dilemmas in young people's lives, his voice can help them to move on and fulfill their own dreams. Hopefully, because of his gift, he will inspire a whole new generation of Chicano and Chicana writers to discover and explore their own gifts.

CHRONOLOGY

1952 Gary Soto is born in Fresno, California, on April 12.

1957 Soto's father, Manuel Soto, dies.

1970 Soto enters Fresno City College as a geography major.

1972 Soto transfers to California State University at Fresno and changes major to English.

1973 *The Iowa Review* accepts Soto's poem for publication, beginning his career as a poet.

1974 Soto graduates magna cum laude from California State University at Fresno with a bachelor of arts degree in English.

1975 Soto marries Carolyn Oda.

1976 Soto graduates from the University of California, Irvine, with an MFA in creative writing.

1977 *The Elements of San Joaquin*, Soto's first book of poems, is published.

1978 Mariko Heidi, Soto's daughter, is born.

1985 Soto becomes associate Professor of English and Chicano studies at the University of California, Berkeley; he teaches there until 1995; Soto's first work of nonfiction, *Living Up the Street*, wins the American Book Award.

1990 Soto's first two books for young readers are published: one collection of poetry, *A Fire in My Hands*, and one collection of short stories, *Baseball in April and Other Stories*.

1995 *Chato's Kitchen*, one of Gary's most popular titles for beginning readers, is published.

2000 *Jessie de la Cruz: A Portrait of a United Farm Worker* allows Soto to tell de la Cruz's story and that of the United Farm Workers to readers everywhere.

2007 Published one new book of poetry for adults, *A Simple Plan.*

NOTES

Chapter 1

1 Rudolfo Anaya, "Gary Soto of the United States," *World Literature Today*, November 2002, www.222.ou.edu/worldlit/NSK/Soto.html.

2 Diane Roback, "Review of *Baseball in April*," *Publisher's Weekly*, March 30, 1990.

3 *Macmillan Profiles: Latino Americans*, New York: Macmillan Library Reference, 1999.

4 "Gary Soto Biography," *Scholastic Books*, Author Studies Homepage, www.scholastic.com/teachers/authorsandbooks/authorstudies/authorhome.jhtml?authorID=89&colla.

5 Gary Soto, *New and Selected Poems*, San Francisco: Chronicle Books, 1995, back cover.

6 Susan Marie Swanson, "Gary Soto," *Riverbank Review*, Fall 1999, pp. 16–18.

7 Gary Soto, *Junior College*, San Francisco: Chronicle Books, 1997, back cover.

8 "Review of *Buried Onions*," *Kirkus Reviews*, August 1, 1997, p. 1229.

9 Gary Soto, *Living Up the Street*, New York: Laurel Leaf Books, 1985, back cover.

10 Don Lee, "About Gary Soto: A Profile," *Ploughshares*, Spring 1995, www.pshares.org/issues/article.cfm?prmArticleid=3863.

11 Hector Torres, *Dictionary of Literary Biography, Volume 82: Chicano Writers*, Detroit, MI: Gale, 1989.

Chapter 2

1 Soto, *Living Up the Street*, p. 2.

2 Dennis Abrams, "Phone Interview with Gary Soto," October 16, 2006.

3 Ibid.

4 Ibid.

5 Ibid.

6 Ibid.

7 Ibid.

8 Gary Soto, *The Effects of Knut Hamsun on a Fresno Boy*, New York: Persea Books, 2000, p. 68.

9 Ibid.

Chapter 3

1 Gary Soto, "Biographical Handout."

2 "An Interview with Gary Soto," http://book.scholastic.com/teachers/authorsandbooks/authorstudies/authorhome.jsp?authorID=89&display/Name=Interview%20Transcripton.

3 Lee, "About Gary Soto," www.pshares.org/issues/article.cfm?prmArticleid=3863.

4 Abrams, "Phone Interview," October 16, 2006.

5 Ibid.

6 "Biography of Gary Soto," www.bookrags.com/Gary_Soto.

7 Soto, *Living Up the Street*, p. 33.

8 Abrams, "Phone Interview," October 16, 2006.

9 Ibid.

10 Ibid.

11 Ibid.

12 Soto, *The Effects of Knut Hamsun on a Fresno Boy*, p. 123.

13 Abrams, "Phone Interview," October 16, 2006.

14 Soto, *Living Up the Street,* p. 73.

15 Abrams, "Phone Interview," October 16, 2006.

16 Ibid.

17 Soto, "Biographical Handout."

18 Abrams, "Phone Interview," October 16, 2006.

19 Soto, "Biographical Handout."

20 Abrams, "Phone Interview," October 16, 2006.

21 Ibid.

22 John Arem, "Interview with Gary Soto," *The Pedestal Magazine*, www.pedestalmagazine.com/secure/content/cb.asp?cbid=2474.

23 Soto, *Living Up the Street*, p. 117.

24 Abrams, "Phone Interview," October 16, 2006.

Chapter 4

1 "Unpublished Interview with Gary Soto," Gary Soto Biography, www.bookrags.com/Gary_Soto.

2 Lee, "About Gary Soto," www.pshares.org/issues/article.cfm?prmArticleid=3863.

3 "Biography," www.bookrags.com/Gary_Soto.

4 Thy Pham and Camile Orillaneda, "Interview with Gary Soto," *Quill* Web site, http://mpnet.esuhsd.org/quill2003/132.pdf, May 7, 2003.

5 Ibid.

6 "Gary Soto Biography," www.bookrags.com/Gary_Soto.

7 Lee, "About Gary Soto," www.pshares.org/issues/article.cfm?prmArticleid=3863.

8 Abrams, "Phone Interview," October 16, 2006.

9 Ibid.

10 Soto, *The Effects of Knut Hamsun on a Fresno Boy*, pp. 44–45.

11 Soto, *The Effects of Knut Hamsun on a Fresno Boy*, p. 46.

12 Soto, "Biographical Handout."

13 Soto, *The Effects of Knut Hamsun on a Fresno Boy*, p. 47.

Chapter 5

1 Gary Soto, "Frequently Asked Questions," www.garysoto.com/faq.html.

2 Lee, "About Gary Soto," www.pshares.org/issues/article.cfm?prmArticleid=3863.

3 Abrams, "Phone Interview," October 16, 2006.

4 Ibid.

5 John Bruce-Nova, *Chicano Poetry: A Response to* Chaos, Austin: University of Texas Press, 1982. Quoted in "Gary Soto Biography," www.bookrags.com/Gary_Soto.

6 Soto, *The Effects of Knut Hamsun on a Fresno Boy*, p. 186.

7 Arthur Ramirez, "Gary Soto," *Revista Chicano-Riguena*, Summer 1981, cited at www.bookrags.com/Gary_Soto.

8 "Gary Soto Biography," www.bookrags.com/Gary_Soto.

9 Ellen Lesser, "Review of *Black Hair*," *Voice Literary Supplement*, September 1985.

10 Tom D'Evelyn, "Review of *Black Hair*," *Christian Science Monitor*, March 6, 1985.

11 Gary Soto, *New and Selected Poems*, San Francisco: Chronicle Books, 1995, p. 72.

12 Ken Shulman, "Bloom and Doom," *Newsweek*, October 10, 1994, p. 75.

13 Dennis Abrams, "E-mail Interview with Gary Soto," October 8, 2006.

14 Lee, "About Gary Soto," www.pshares.org/issues/article.cfm?prmArticleid=3863.

15 Francisco Aragon, "An Interview with Gary Soto," Institute for Latino Studies, Momotombo Press, www.nd.edu/~latino/momotombo/soto_interview.html.

16 Ibid.

Chapter 6

1 Thinkquest, "Literary Terms," library.thinkquest.org/23846/library/terms/index.html.

2 Abrams, "Phone Interview," October 16, 2006.

3 Abrams, "E-mail Interview," September 30, 2006.

4 Ibid.

5 Lee, "About Gary Soto," www.pshares.org/issues/article.cfm?prmArticleid=3863.

6 Soto, "Biographical Handout."

7 "Unpublished Interview," Gary Soto Biography, www.bookrags.com/Gary_Soto.

8 Geoffrey Dunn, "Review of *Living Up the Street*," *San Francisco Review of Books*, Summer 1986, p. 11.

9 Alicia Fields, "Small But Telling Moments," *Bloomsbury Review*, January-February, 1987, p. 10.

10 "Gary Soto Biography," www.bookrags.com/Gary_Soto.

11 Ernesto Trejo, "Memories of a Fresno Boyhood," *Los Angeles Times Book Review*, August 5, 1998, pp. 1, 9.

12 "Gary Soto Biography," *Booklist Biography*, www.notablebiographies.com/news/sh-z/soto-gary.html.

Chapter 7

1 "Gary Soto Biography," *Booklist Biography*, www.notablebiographies.com/news/sh-z/soto-gary.html.

2 Gary Soto, "On the Particulars of the World," in *Literature for Today's Young Adults*, Kenneth L. Donelson and Alleen Pace, eds. Boston: Allyn and Bacon, 2005.

3 Abrams, "E-mail Interview," October 8, 2006.

4 Soto, "Biographical Handout."

5 Abrams, "Phone Interview," October 16, 2006.

6 "Review of *Baseball in April and Other Stories*," *Los Angeles Times Book Review*.

7 Book of the Month: Gary Soto, *Baseball in April*, www.mhhe.com/soscience/education/kidlit/bom/nov2000_bom.html.

8 Ibid.

9 Roger Sutton, "Review of *Baseball in April*," *Bulletin for the Center for Children's Books*, April 1990, p. 199.

10 Soto, *Effects of Knut Hamsun on a Fresno Boy*, p. 185.

11 "Review of *Taking Sides*," *Kirkus Reviews*, September 15, 1991, p. 1228.

12 Bruce Anne Shook, "Review of *Taking Sides*," *School Library Journal*, November 1991, p. 124.

13 Ellen Fader, "Review of *Pacific Crossing*," *Horn Book*, November-December 1992, pp. 725-26.

14 "Review of *Buried Onions*," *Kirkus Reviews*, August 1, 1997, p. 1229.

15 Abrams, "Phone Interview," October 16, 2006.

16 "Interview with Gary Soto," Harcourt Trade Publishers, www.harcourtbooks.com/authorinterviews/bookinterview_Soto.asp.

17 Ibid.

18 "A Review of *The Afterlife*," *Publisher's Weekly*, August 25, 2003, http://reviews.publibsher-sweekly.com/bd.aspx?isbn=0152047743&pub=pw.

19 Joel Shoemaker, "Review of *Jesse*," *School Library Journal*, cited at www.amazon.com.

20 Merri Monks, "Review of *Jesse*," *Booklist,* cited at www.amazon.com.

21 Abrams, "Phone Interview," October 16, 2007.

22 "A Review of *Crazy Weekend*," *Publisher's Weekly*, 1994, www.amazon.com.

23 Dona Weisman, "Review of *Local News*," *School Library Journal*, 1993, cited at www.amazon.com.

24 Abrams, "Phone Interview," October 16, 2006.

25 Gary Soto, *Help Wanted*, New York: Harcourt, Inc., 2005, p. 134.

26 Ibid.

27 Ibid.

28 Ann Welton, "A Review of *Chato and the Party Animals*," *School Library Journal*, cited at www.amazon.com.

29 Renee Steinberg, "Review of *Neighborhood Odes*," *School Library Journal*, May 1992, p. 128.

30 Gary Soto, *Canto Familiar*, New York: Harcourt Brace & Company, 1995, p. 31.

31 Abrams, "Phone Interview," October 16, 2006.

Chapter 8

1 Abrams, "Phone Interview," October 16, 2006.

2 Ibid.

3 Ibid.

4 *Contemporary Literary Criticism*, Volume 80, p. 275.

5 Abrams, "Phone Interview," October 16, 2006.

6 Ibid.

7 Abrams, "E-mail Interview," September 30, 2006.

8 Soto, *The Effects of Knut Hamsun on a Fresno Boy,* pp. 200–201.

9 Ibid.

10 Abrams, "E-mail Interview," September 30, 2006.

11 "Unpublished Interview," Gary Soto Biography, www.bookrags.com/Gary_Soto.

WORKS BY GARY SOTO

FOR CHILDREN AND YOUNG ADULTS

Poetry

1991 *A Fire in My Hands*

1992 *Neighborhood Odes*

1997 *Canto Familiar*

2002 *Fearless Fernie: Hanging Out With Fernie and Me*

2005 *Worlds Apart*

2006 *A Fire in My Hands, Expanded Edition*

Fiction

1990 *Baseball in April and Other Stories*

1991 *Taking Sides*; *Pacific Crossing*

1992 *The Skirt*

1993 *Too Many Tamales*; *Local News*; *The Pool Party*

1994 *Jesse*; *Crazy Weekend*

1995 *Chato's Kitchen*; *Summer on Wheels*; *Off and Running*; *Boys at Work*

1996 *Old Man and His Door*

1997 *Snapshots From the Wedding*

1998 *Buried Onions*; *Big Bushy Mustache*

2000 *Chato and the Party Animals*

2002 *If the Shoe Fits*

2003 *The Afterlife*

2005 *Help Wanted*; *Chato Goes Cruisin'*

2006 *Accidental Love*; *My Little Car/Mi Carrito*

2007 *Mercy on These Teenage Chimps*

2008 (in press) *Facts of Life*

Biography

2000 *Jessie de la Cruz: The Life and Times of a United Farm Worker*

2003 *Cesar Chavez: A Hero for Everyone*

Plays and Films

1993 *The Pool Party*

1997 *Novio Boy*

1999 *Nerdlandia*

BOOKS FOR ADULTS

Poetry

1977 *The Elements of San Joaquin*

1978 *The Tale of Sunlight*

1981 *Where Sparrows Work Hard*

1985 *Black Hair*

1990 *Who Will Know Us?*

1991 *Home Course in Religion*

1995 *New and Selected Poems*

1997 *Junior College*

1999 *A Natural Man*

2003 *One Kind of Faith*

2007 *A Simple Plan*

Personal Essays

1988 *Lesser Evils*; *California Childhood* (editor)

1990 *A Summer Life*

1992 *Living Up the Street*

1993 *Small Faces*

2000 *The Effects of Knut Hamsun on a Fresno Boy*

Fiction

1993 *Pieces of the Heart: New Chicano Short Fiction* (editor)

2000 *Nickel and Dime*

2001 *Poetry Lover*

2003 *Amnesia in a Republican Country*

POPULAR BOOKS

BASEBALL IN APRIL AND OTHER STORIES

This collection of short stories is Soto's first work for young readers. The stories show the everyday life of Mexican-American kids growing up in California's Central Valley, but their themes are universal.

BURIED ONIONS

This novel tells the story of 19-year-old Eddie, living in the barrio but desperate to make a better life for himself. When his cousin is murdered, his cousin's mother asks Eddie to take revenge. He must make major decisions that will affect his entire life.

CHATO'S KITCHEN

Chato the cat and his best friend, Novio Boy, invite a family of mice to dinner—expecting the mice themselves to become dinner! When the mice arrive, though, they bring along a surprise that changes everything.

NEIGHBORHOOD ODES

This collection of poems for young readers describes ordinary life in the neighborhood: playing under the sprinkler, eating a warm buttered tortilla, and lifting weights, among others. The poems reveal the poetry and the magic that surround the most common of everyday events.

NOVIO BOY

Soto's funniest and most popular play examines the world of dating from both male and female perspectives. When Patricia, a high school junior, agrees to go to lunch with ninth grader Rudy, nearly everything that can go wrong does.

TAKING SIDES

Lincoln Mendoza has moved with his mom from the urban barrio of the Mission District in San Francisco to a mostly Anglo suburban community. There, he finds himself torn between old and new friends, his old basketball team and his new school's team, and his old way of life versus his new one.

POPULAR CHARACTERS

CHATO

Chato is the coolest, hippest cat in Los Angeles. He and his best buddy, Novio Boy, bring a cat's eye view to the colorful life of the barrio.

EDDIE

The hero of *Buried Onions*, Eddie is an ornery but ultimately decent guy who has been scarred by life in the barrio. He would like nothing more than to escape and find a better life for himself, but events conspire to make such dreams nearly impossible.

LINCOLN MENDOZA

Smart and athletic, Lincoln learns to deal with moving from the barrio to an Anglo suburb in *Taking Sides*. He also stars in the book *Pacific Crossing*, in which he and his friend Tony go to Japan as exchange students and face new cultural challenges.

MAJOR AWARDS

1975 "Discovery," *The Nation*, the Joan Leiman Jacobson Poetry Prize

1976 The United States Award from the International Poetry Forum

1978 Bess Hokin Prize from *Poetry*

1979 Guggenheim Fellowship

1981 NEA Fellowship for Creative Writers

1984 Levinson Prize from *Poetry*

1985 Before Columbus Foundation American Book Award for *Living Up the Street*

1989 California Arts Council Fellowship

1990 The American Library Association's Best Book for Young Adults Award for *Baseball in April and Other Stories*

1991 California Library Association's John and Patricia Beatty Award for *Baseball in April and Other Stories*; NEA Fellowship for Creative Writers

1993 Recognition of Merit from the George G. Stone Center, Claremont Graduate School for *Baseball in April and Other Stories*; Andrew Carnegie Medal for the film *The Pool Party*

1995 Finalist for the *Los Angeles Times* Book Award for *New and Selected Poems*

1996 The Tomas Rivera Prize for *Chato's Kitchen*; The California Library Association's John and Patricia Beatty Award for *Summer on Wheels*

1999 PEN West Center Book Award for *Petty Crimes*; Human and Civil Rights Award from the National Education Association; Literature Award from the Hispanic Heritage Foundation

2001 Young People's Ambassador for California Rural Legal Assistance (CRLA) and the United Farm Workers of America (UFW)

BIBLIOGRAPHY

Abrams, Dennis. "E-mail Interview with Gary Soto." September 30, 2006.

———. "E-mail Interview with Gary Soto." October 8, 2006.

———. "Phone Interview with Gary Soto." October 16, 2006.

Amen, John. "Interview with Gary Soto." *The Pedestal Magazine.com.*

Aragon, Francisco. "An Interview with Gary Soto." Momotombo Press, July-August 2005.

Gale Reference Team. "Biography—Soto, Gary (1952–). *Contemporary Authors*, Thomson Gale, 2004.

Ganz, Robin. "Gary Soto." *Updating the Literary West*. Texas Christian University Press, 1997, pp. 426–433.

Lee, Gary. "About Gary Soto: A Profile." *Ploughshares*, Spring 1993.

Monks, Merri. "Review of *Jesse.*" *Booklist.*

Orr, Tamra. *Gary Soto*. New York: The Rosen Publishing Group, 2005.

"Review of *The Afterlife*," *Publishers Weekly*, August 8, 2005.

Shoemaker, Joel. "Review of *Jesse*," *School Library Journal*, 1994.

Shulman, Ken. "Bloom and Doom." *Newsweek*, October 10, 1994, p. 75.

Soto, Gary. "Biographical Handout."

———. "On the Particulars of the World," in *Literature for Today's Young Adults*, Kenneth L. Donelson and Alleen Pace, eds. Boston: Allyn and Bacon, 2005.

———. "Frequently Asked Questions," www.garysoto.com/faq.html.

———. *Buried Onions*. New York: HarperCollins Publishers, 1999.

———. *Canto Familiar*. San Diego and New York: Harcourt Brace & Company, 1995.

———. *The Effects of Knut Hamsun on a Fresno Boy*. New York: Persea Books, 2000.

———. *Help Wanted*. New York: Harcourt Inc., 2005.

———. *Living Up the Street*. New York: Laurel Leaf Books, 1985.

———. *New and Selected Poems*. San Francisco: Chronicle Books, 1995.

Steinberg, Renee. "Review of *Neighborhood Odes*," *School Library Journal*, 1992.

Welton, Ann. "Review of *Chato and the Party Animal*." *School Library Journal*, 2000.

Web Sites

Excerpts from Reviews. McGraw-Hill Higher Education Web site. Available online. URL: www.mhhe.com/socscience/education/kidlit/bom/nov2000_bom.htm.

Gary Soto Biography. Available online. URL: www.bookrags.com.

Gary Soto Biography: Life in the Barrio, Poet of the People. Available online. URL: www.notablebiographies.com/news/Sh-Z/Soto-Gary.html.

Gary Soto's Interview Transcript, *Scholastic Books***.** Available online. URL: http://books.scholastic.com/teachers/authorsandbooks/authorstudies/authorhome.jsp?authorID=89&display/Name=Interview%20Transcript.

Interview with Gary Soto. Harcourt Trade Publishers Web site. Available online. URL: www.harcourtbooks.com/authorinterviews/bookinterview_Soto.asp.

FURTHER READING

Allen, Donald. *The New American Poetry.* Berkeley: University of California Press, 1999.

Atkin, S. Beth. *Voices From the Fields: Children of Migrant Farmworkers Tell Their Stories*. Boston: Little Brown, 2000.

Braithwaite, E.R. *To Sir with Love*, reissue edition. Jove, 1990.

Burns, Olive Ann, *Cold Sassy Tree*. Boston: Mariner Books, 2007.

Jimenez, Victor, *The Circuit: Stories from the Life of a Migrant Child*. New York: Houghton Mifflin, 1999.

Martinez, Victor, *Parrot in the Oven: Mi Vida*, reprint edition. New York: Rayo, 2004.

Web Sites

Gary Soto Official Site
www.garysoto.com

Poem Hunter
www.poemhunter.com

United Farm Workers official site
www.ufw.org

PICTURE CREDITS

page:

10: AP Images, Tina Ramirez
15: Courtesy of Gary Soto
18: AP Images, Marcio Jose Sanchez
23: Courtesy of Gary Soto
28: Courtesy of Gary Soto
37: AP Images, Susan Sterner
44: Courtesy of California State University at Fresno
49: AP Images, Gary Kazanjian
51: AP Images, Sakuma
54: Courtesy of Gary Soto
66: Bantam/Dell. Photo by Spring Mount Photography
72: Getty Images
74: Harcourt, Inc. Photo by Spring Mount Photography
81: Scholastic, Inc. Photo by Spring Mount Photography
94: Courtesy of Gary Soto
98: Harcourt, Inc. Photo by Spring Mount Photography

Cover: Carolyn Soto

The excerpt from "On the Particulars of the World" that appears on pages 76–77 was reprinted by the permission of Gary Soto.

INDEX

ABOUT THE AUTHOR

DENNIS ABRAMS is the author of numerous books for Chelsea House, including biographies of Barbara Park, Hamid Karzai, Ty Cobb, and Eminem. He attended Antioch College, where he majored in English and communications. He currently resides in Houston with his partner of 18 years, along with their two dogs and three cats.